CANADIAN KINDNESS
IN THE FACE OF COVID-19

NOT CANCELLED

CANADIAN KINDESS
IN THE FACE OF COVID-19

HEATHER DOWN & CATHERINE KENWELL

echo
BOOKS

Wintertickle PRESS

Wintertickle Press
132 Commerce Park Drive,
Unit K, Ste. 155
Barrie, ON, L4N 0Z7

wintericklepress.com
FB/wintericklepress

Library and Archives Canada Cataloguing in Publication

Title: Not cancelled : Canadian kindness in the face of COVID-19 / Heather Down & Catherine Kenwell.
Names: Down, Heather, 1966- editor. | Kenwell, Catherine, 1962- editor.
Description: Edited by Heather Down and Catherine Kenwell.
Identifiers: Canadiana (print) 20200242849 | Canadiana (ebook) 20200242997 | ISBN 9781989664025 (softcover) | ISBN 9781989664032 (EPUB) | ISBN 9781989664049 (Kindle)
Subjects: LCSH: Coronavirus infections—Social aspects—Canada—History—21st century. | LCSH: Epidemics—Social aspects—Canada—History—21st century. | LCSH: Quarantine—Social aspects—Canada—History—21st century. | LCSH: Coronavirus infections—Canada—History—21st century. | LCSH: Epidemics—Canada—History—21st century. | LCSH: Quarantine—Canada—History—21st century.

Classification: LCC RA643.7.C3 N68 2020 | DDC 362.1962—dc23

This book is a labour of love and dedicated to:

*our front-line workers—from health care to essential service
providers, thank you for being our superheroes
and keeping us safe;*

*friends and families of those who have lost loved ones
during the pandemic;*

*our community leaders, who have navigated the unknown with
care and compassion;*

and to

RCMP Const. Heidi Stevenson
Greg and Jamie Blair
Lisa McCully
Heather O'Brien
Alanna Jenkins and Sean McLeod
Jolene Oliver, Emily Tuck, and Aaron (Friar) Tuck
Frank Gulenchyn and Dawn Madsen
Gina Goulet
Lillian Hyslop
Tom Bagley
Kristen Beaton and her unborn baby
John Zahl and Elizabeth Joanne Thomas
Corrie Ellison
Joey Webber
Joy and Peter Bond

We grieve as one; we are inspired by many. We are Canada.

TABLE OF CONTENTS

COVID
BE
GONE

By Carter Mann, Sudbury, age eleven

COVID be gone in the depths of dawn
May we rise to be infection free
The isolated days so many are feeling
Our minds sit in darkness and are in need of healing
Our leaders work tirelessly to bring us comfort
As the death toll rises, we grieve with such loss
Distancing from our loved ones we carry our cross
The days seem endless with so full of despair
Where is the light, with no end in sight
The darkness we must overcome
Stand strong and fight as a world we must become one

INTRODUCTION

LIKE MANY GOOD IDEAS, THIS book was inspired by a Facebook post. I had been thinking about compiling an anthology of human-interest stories about the unprecedented times we as Canadians were facing during COVID-19. I just hadn't formulated the exact approach. I knew this was not only a time of deep reflection for our nation but also a significant moment in social history, full of storytelling and events that also should be recorded—something to show the great-grandkids one day. I had a vague framework but no specific plan of attack. And then I saw a post from fellow author Catherine Kenwell: **Laughter Is Not Cancelled.**

A eureka moment! I approached her. "Want to do a book about positive stories? We can collect reflections and write third-person accounts. I love your post. In a time when it feels like lots of things are being cancelled—sports, concerts, recreation, and nights out with friends—maybe we could focus on everything that is still happening, call it *Not Cancelled.*"

"Yes, yes, and yes! Let's do it."

So the birth of a book about goodness in a time of darkness was born. Don't get me wrong, this is not a slight to the serious heaviness of COVID-19. This isn't a dismissive book filled with rainbows and unicorns, stories that attempt to diminish the grim reality. Both Catherine and I have personally been affected by the ramifications this virus and lockdown bring. We have experienced loss, and funerals either never happened at all or were held virtually. Mourning together yet apart leaves permanent scars on your soul.

As I write this, my own aunt, my father's only sister, lies in a long-term care facility, diagnosed with the novel coronavirus. She is ninety-three, and dementia prevents her from being able to talk to her loved ones on the phone. As of today, she has neither succumbed to the virus nor recovered from it—the ending to this chapter not yet written. There is no doubt this is a heart-wrenching time.

Catherine, too, has been knocked down enough to appreciate every day on this side of the grass—in fact, her past traumas have given her a unique perspective on gratitude in the face of adversity. While her first defence is often humour, she has also mourned the loss of family and friends during this pandemic. Two of her mother's siblings died within one week—both of them in long-term care homes. In sharing her own observations, she speaks for others who have a difficult time articulating their fears and anxieties.

It could be said that this project saved us. The often-quoted Mr. Rogers ("look for the helpers") buoyed our mental health. In the weeks of lockdown, both Catherine and I had little, if any, control over our mood swings. We seriously wondered if the next DSM (*Diagnostic and Statistical Manual of Mental Disorders*) would include an emerging new condition, a coronavirus-induced mood disorder. Our emotional dysregulation would take us from unearthly optimism to hellish despair in split seconds.

Luckily, we would have the pleasure of conducting phone interviews with Canadians across this amazing country. We "met" so many beautiful people who simply lifted our spirits in a time when we needed it most. From a dancing Sikh in the Yukon to a couple's first wedding dance in British Columbia to a talking schnauzer in Quebec to a real-life Spider-Man walking the streets of Newfoundland, we realized that, for the most part, Canadians are kind, creative, and ultimately, resilient. This project gave us a glimmer of hope.

Then came the tragedy in Nova Scotia: an epic crisis within an epic crisis. Grief compounded by mandated isolation. No words can express the resulting level of sadness and trauma. To the victims, to the families, to the province, and to the country: know our hearts collectively bleed.

If ever there is a time we could use a ray of sunshine, it is now. It is both Catherine's and my hope to lift up this nation we love so dearly and share this anthology with you.

After writing many stories and collecting others—forty-nine in all, representing Canada's address of the forty-ninth parallel—

the challenge was how to combine so many voices, styles, and approaches to create one cohesive book. Stories came from every single province, spanning Indigenous people to new immigrants—and everybody whose family has occupied this country in a time frame in between. We acknowledged Canada's diversity, and we realized that our collective voices can have variation but still sing the same tune. You will find narratives, reflections, past-tense and present-tense essays, polished literary pieces, and stories from newly minted writers who are sharing their souls the best they can. Like a maple tree, consisting of various roots, branches, and foliage, these parts make the perfect whole, just like the country its leaf represents.

Please keep in mind that the public health rules changed rapidly as we moved along in this journey of COVID-19. Be cognizant that some stories were told from times before travel restrictions and social distancing—and may seem reckless from our vantage point of experience. Just remember the authors were following the directives of the time.

When the country was first thrust into lockdown, it seemed like everything was being cancelled. But, upon reflection, important things like love, kindness, hope, joy, and humour were certainly *Not Cancelled.*

LAUGHTER IS NOT CANCELLED

BY CATHERINE KENWELL

THIS MORNING, MY HUSBAND AND I were having coffee and watching a bit of *Your Morning*, our regular morning news and entertainment TV. An expert was offering up new ways to keep kids occupied, active, and learning while they're at home. She said something to the effect of:

"Give kids a measuring tape and have them measure their bedrooms, and then ask them how they'd redecorate the space. Or, get them to measure out the backyard, and then figure out what they could fit into it."

Kevin pipes up: "My Mom did that when I was a kid!"

"She had you measure the backyard . . . at the cottage? Wow!" My eyes widen with awe.

Now, the cottage had a huge backyard, and there were no fences for miles, so effectively the job was an endless one. Kevin spent entire summers at the cottage. *Good thing*, I consider. *Kudos to a clever mom*. The uncontrollable laughter was starting to roil in my belly.

Without pausing, he replies, "Yeah, and she only gave me a twelve-inch ruler!"

"And she told you not to come home until you were done?"

I almost spit out my coffee as the laughter boils over.

"And then I had to measure the lake!" he adds.

Dying now.

"What, like from the bottom?"

We're both gasping between howls.

"Yeah, it was a drag when I forgot and had to start all over again!"

Laughter is a gift and a healer. I hope this lightens your day. Keep safe, friends.

Catherine Kenwell is a Barrie, Ontario, author and qualified mediator. Her works have been featured in Chicken Soup for the Soul, Brainstorm Revolution, *and several international horror anthologies. She is currently working on a horror novel and an autobiographical brain-injury memoir.*

THE TOOTH FAIRY IS NOT CANCELLED

By Heather Down with Tania Marsh
& Jacqueline Pennington

TANIA, A NURSE AT A local hospital, felt her anxiety rise with the curve of the pandemic. This single mother was the primary caregiver for her two girls ages twelve and fifteen, and she didn't want to take any chances of exposing her family to COVID-19. Her oldest had severe asthma, and her parents, who lived in a nanny suite in her home, were in a higher-risk category as well.

While talking to her best friend, Tania mentioned, "I am not sure what I should do. I have been hearing that some health care workers are testing positive for the coronavirus. To minimize the risk to their families, others are stripping off in their garages and showering as soon as they get home."

"That is an option," her friend replied.

"Yeah, I guess so. I would probably have more peace of mind if I could self-isolate from my family."

This sparked an idea in her friend. "Hey, what about a trailer?"

"That's not a bad idea, you know. I have a seasonal trailer at a campground not too far away."

Tania called the campground. "Hi. Are you guys open for people to use their trailer and just go back and forth to work?"

"Sorry. We have shut down completely: no tenants at all for any reason."

"I totally understand," she replied.

Hmmm, maybe I could rent a trailer and keep it in the drive-way, Tania thought. Buoyed by this potential solution, she called around. But rental companies had either ceased renting or were too cost prohibitive.

Tania turned to social media and posted:

> Wondering if anyone has a small camper that I can use in my driveway to live in while I have to return to work and I don't want to bring home this virus to my girls. My oldest has bad asthma and my parents are living in the basement apartment. I don't know if I'm overthinking or being way too prepared but I would rather that than ever have regrets. I am not directly looking after COVID patients yet. But it may be just a matter of time in the next couple weeks. I welcome suggestions from friends or solutions to my situation. I am the primary caregiver for my girls. And they need to stay safe here at home.

AN HOUR'S DRIVE AWAY IN the little town of Grafton, Ontario, an article on Facebook caught the eye of real estate agent Jacqueline. She clicked on the link to learn about a doctor in the United States. His wife had erected a tent in the garage for her husband to sleep in to reduce the chance of coronavirus exposure to the family. The article highlighted the abundant challenges facing front-line health care workers. They were going into hospitals; they were potentially exposing themselves to the virus. However, they did not want to risk the safety of their families.

Jacqueline was reading this article about a week before things were going to get very real in Canada. She realized this country was not going to be immune to this pandemic.

"Greg," she called out to her husband. "I have an idea . . ."

Greg and Jacqueline had purchased a brand-new camper trailer the year before. They hadn't even had a chance to use it yet. It sat empty in their garage.

"What's your idea?" Greg queried.

"We are so lucky. We get to stay in our homes and not have to worry day in and day out if we will bring in something that can hurt our children. What about our front-line health care workers? We don't know what they face every day and the worry they must have around keeping their own families safe. The stress of it all probably also affects their mental health."

Greg nodded in agreement.

"What if we offered our trailer to a front-line worker who might want to isolate from their family? They could borrow it during the crisis?"

There was no question this was what they should do, and Jacqueline posted her offer in a local Facebook group, not knowing if anyone would actually respond.

TANIA RECEIVED A MESSAGE WITH a link from her friend that simply said: **Check this out**. She read the message and quickly contacted Jacqueline to see if the trailer was still available.

In a matter of days, Greg delivered the camper, plugged it in, hooked up the water, wiped everything down, and showed Tania around.

She wanted to hug him but instead kept her physical distance. "Please, at least take this gas card," she said.

"No, I won't take it," he insisted. "Just go to work, be safe, and do for us what we can't do for others. You are a front-line worker with the qualifications and skills that I don't have. I can't care for others the way that you can." Tania tried not to tear up.

After Greg left, Tania looked around in amazement. Besides a beautiful trailer, an oasis that could help keep her family safe, she noticed the "welcome home" mat; the stocked fridge filled with frozen soups, granola bars, and treats; the hand sanitizer and disinfectant wipes; and the *pièce de résistance*—toilet paper!

Tania sat for a moment, overwhelmed and grateful. She had worried parents and a mortgage to pay, and she was raising two children. Every emotion hit her all at once. She could not express how this simple selfless act of generosity had affected her. She cried.

The next night Tania ate her supper outside on the deck while her girls ate their dinner inside the house. At least they could see each other through the sliding glass doors. It was their new normal of sharing a meal together. Although the girls missed the physical contact with their mom, they understood why this was happening and that it was for everyone's well-being.

The next morning, Tania heard the front door to her house swing open. "Mom, mom . . ." an excited voice yelled.

Tania opened the trailer door to see her youngest daughter standing within the front-door frame of the house, bursting with good news.

"Yes, honey. What is it?"

"I lost my molar yesterday. I wasn't sure the tooth fairy would come, but I put my tooth under my pillow anyway . . . and guess what?"

"What?" Tania smiled.

"She did. The tooth fairy left a toonie under my pillow!"

Tania grinned, realizing that we are all in this together and that caring has many faces. Whether a stranger with a trailer or a faithful tooth fairy, community can bring a sense of safety and normalcy to us all.

Tania Marsh is a nurse in Belleville, Ontario, where she resides with her two children.

Jacqueline Pennington is a real estate agent in Grafton, Ontario, where she lives with her husband and children.

BIRTHDAYS ARE NOT CANCELLED

By Maud Revel

I ALWAYS LOOK FORWARD TO the last week of March. You see, I have lots to celebrate at the end of March. Spring has officially arrived (if you trust the calendar), snow is gone (most of the time), and I start spotting green things in the yard. And in my household, there are three birthdays to celebrate: my soon-to-be husband's, mine, and my business's. We all vary in age, but we group them together for a generous serving of cake.

This year is a little different, though, as all of us in Canada are on self-imposed or mandated confinement to help slow down the progression of this COVID-19 pandemic. Sure enough, spring has arrived, the snow is gone, and green things are sprouting. But there is a bit of a gloomy cloud hanging over our heads. We are following government recommendations and social distancing from friends and family. This new term has become a verb quite quickly and turned into a new way of life. Tough adjustment for yours truly, coming from a French background of cheek kissing (by the way, the mystery remains as to when to exchange one, two, three, or even four cheek kisses) and having embraced, quite literally, the Canadian hugging practice. I love a good, strong, heartfelt hug! More than I love butter tarts from the local Sweet Oven, which makes the best butter tarts in the county . . . or is it country?

So here we are, the last week of March, with no hug in sight. I guess I will turn to cake. My other half's birthday comes first, mine follows a few days later, and we top off the week with my business's. This year we tally seventy-nine years. In my craving for comfort, chocolate cake comes to mind. So I open the recipe book my mother made for my thirtieth birthday, gathering childhood photographs and family recipes that she took the time to write by hand. My mother has a beautiful, teacher-like handwriting; couple it with a wide-tip calligraphy pen and I am the lucky owner of a work of art. There are quite a few chocolate cake recipes in the family, some with cocoa, some with chocolate, some with flour, some without. As I read through them all, memories of various family events come to mind. I settle for my cousin's flourless recipe, and I smile as I recall how I came to obtain this particular recipe.

About fifteen years ago when I lived in Germany, my cousin was just on the other side of the border in Strasbourg, France, so I visited him regularly to recharge my French batteries. This particular visit was the last week of March. He had no idea it was my birthday, and I never reminded him because I was just happy with the company. He decided to bake this chocolate cake, whipped it up in minutes, and proceeded to put it in the oven. We got talking about this and that, catching up on life, family matters, and . . . *what is that smell?* Something is burning! It dawns on us that he never set a timer. Smoke is coming out of the oven, and our chocolate cake is quite dark. Not ones to be deterred, and determined to have cake, we simply cut the top layer off and enjoy a moist, tasty chocolate cake christened "the almost birthday cake."

I believe this is the perfect memory. An almost birthday cake for three birthdays without being able to invite company should defy the gloom. Add to that the fact that it requires only five ingredients, which I happen to have in the house. *Score!* Baking makes me smile. Step into the kitchen with me . . .

Almost Birthday Cake
200 g of baking chocolate (that would be 8 squares for non-metric folks)
125 g of butter (1/2 cup)
6 eggs
125 g of sugar (1/2 cup)
A pinch of salt

Turn the oven on to 400 degrees Fahrenheit, then pull out a square 9 x 9 cake pan (a 9- or 10-inch round one will do, too), two large bowls, a whisk, and two pots. One pot needs to fit into the other. Fill the larger pot with about a quarter to a third of water, just enough to allow the smaller pot to sit in water. Break the chocolate squares into the smaller pan and put on the stove. You are creating a water bath to melt the chocolate without burning it.

While this is going, separate the yolks from the whites in the two large bowls that you have set out. Add the sugar to the yolks and whisk into a smooth paste. Add the pinch of salt to the whites and beat them into a stiff-peaked mousse. When the chocolate is melted, add the butter cut in chunks. Leave the mix on the water bath until the butter is melted and then mix it into the chocolate. Don't forget to taste . . . it's part of the recipe.

Slowly pour the melted chocolate and butter into the yolks and sugar so as to not cook the eggs, whisking gently to combine. Make sure you scrape off all the chocolate from the pot and lick the spoon before you wash it. No point in wasting any of the chocolate, right? You will need patience for the next step. Gently fold the whites into the chocolate mix. Take your time if you want a moist cake. Finally, pour into the buttered and floured cake pan and place in the oven for 20 to 25 minutes. Don't forget to set a timer!

I HAVE TWENTY MINUTES TO wait, so I go back to the office to answer some emails. The lovely smell of chocolate starts to fill the house. My nose tells me the twenty minutes are up just before the timer goes off. I walk back into the kitchen and arm myself with two oven mitts, ready for battle. I grab the cake and set it on the stove, place a cooling rack on top, and I flip it upside down. Unfortunately, the cake is stuck to the pan, so I flip it back to be able to run a blade along the side. Next thing I know, the pan is slipping out of my hands, and I see myself jumping back to avoid burning my feet.

I start laughing hysterically. My laughter turns into sobs and back into laughter. History is repeating itself . . . This recipe is doomed, the cake aptly named the almost birthday cake. I stare at the disaster lying right in front of me. Half the cake is still in the pan; the other half is on the floor. I have been laughing and crying for a moment now; I can't even pretend to apply the five-second rule. This can't be the end of it. Our birthdays will not be cancelled, and I will not be beaten by a chocolate cake. There is one person I can always call to do a reset, so I pick up the phone and text my sister-in-law. The pictures of the baking disaster have us both buckled over laughing.

But I still need to fix this birthday cake situation. I pull out three ramekins and fill them with what is left of the cake. In the fridge I find a carton of whipping cream. This should do. I pour about a third of a cup into a deep bowl and I start whipping. Right hand . . . then left to take a break . . . back to the right . . . circles, then lateral movements. My mind wanders as I whip the cream. In my daze, my eyes settle on a bottle of Sheridan's coffee liqueur. Chocolate, whipping cream, and coffee should mix well together, right? I pour some liqueur into the cream, whisk it in and taste. Just a little more and taste again. Perfect. I resume whipping the cream, right hand, left hand, circle, lateral, until it is thick and smooth. I set it aside until dinnertime.

I go back to the office and finish my day knowing I can still save these birthdays. Just before dinner, I cover the chocolate cake with enough cream to make a banana split jealous and top up the three servings with a candle. One for my other half, one for me, and one for my business.

Our birthdays will not be cancelled!

Maud Revel is a language teacher, a certified horseback riding instructor, and a level III Equine Assisted Learning facilitator at New Horserizons. She runs horse-led programs designed to create change and awareness in people. Her main programs are tailored for professionals in uniform affected by PTSD; others are designed for couples, families, and aspiring and inspiring leaders. When not at the barn, she can be found reading, taking photographs, or digging a hole in her garden to plant yet another tree or shrub.

JOY IS NOT CANCELLED

By Heather Down with Susan Gaudet
and Christie Stetson

PEI BORN-AND-RAISED SUSAN LOST HER mom when she was only seven years old. She watched her father, a hopeless romantic, try to cope with his grief by turning to photography. He and her mother had been together for over twenty-five years, and the loss was devastating.

Susan's life would not get easier, however. At the age of eighteen, while in her last year of high school, her father passed from cancer. For the first year, Susan appeared to be coping, but soon things started to spin out in a chaotic direction. She felt she was on the wrong path, and without properly processing her losses, she fell into a ten-year depression.

Years later in Calgary, she found herself contemplating her next move—a serious long-term relationship had gone belly-up. While together, her ex had given her a camera, but he kept it when they divided their things.

Without much money or a plan, Susan decided to go back to PEI, even though she didn't have family there anymore. Eventually, she managed to land a job at the local Best Buy.

One day a friend reached out to her. "Hey. I have this camera." Ironically, he was also in the midst of a separation. He had bought his girlfriend a camera, and she didn't want it anymore. "I was going to sell it. Do you want it?"

"Do I want it? Of course. Yes, please!"

Susan started to play around with her camera, dabbling with creative shots for her Instagram account. Never did she imagine another friend would call her and ask, "Would you be comfortable if I recommended you for a wedding?"

Taken aback, she stuttered, "Oh . . . I don't know. I have never done anything like that before."

"It's no big deal. The couple is really low key and mostly just want a casual capturing of the day."

Susan sighed. "Are you sure they are really laid back?"

"Yes, trust me," her friend answered.

"Okay. I will meet with them and see."

The couple was a perfect fit for Susan's style of photography and loved her work. It didn't take long for word to go around how talented Susan was, and one wedding grew into many.

In fact, Susan ended up starting her own business and called it Anita Marie Photography. Anita was her late mother's name, and both of them shared the middle name Marie. She felt this was the perfect title to honour her mother and to also insert a part of herself.

Shortly before flights were restricted into Canada and self-isolation became a common term, Susan was at a photography conference in Joshua Tree, California. She befriended a photographer from Texas.

She came back to Canada, and for a little while things continued as normal. Then the world shifted, almost instantly. Sitting at home, she was scrolling through her Texan photographer-friend's feed and saw a call-out to see if any of her clients would like "front step" photos. The Front Steps Project is a movement where photographers take family portraits on their clients' front step from a safe distance, usually collecting donations for charities.

Hmmm, Susan thought. *This might be a great way to bring some joy during these times and raise some much-needed funds for local food banks and charities.*

She didn't think she would get much of a response, but she threw up the call-out on her Facebook page. It didn't take long for fifty-some families to say they would like to participate.

Susan got organized. She created a safety sheet, outlining her stringent protocols to keep herself and her clients safe with physical distancing (she would be using a telephoto lens to remain a safe distance away), she organized the requests by communities so she could hit up certain areas at once, and she created a schedule.

Payment was optional and hands-free: e-Transfer only. All donated funds went to support those who were food insecure. Susan's new sense of purpose to spread joy was under way.

HIGH SCHOOL ENGLISH TEACHER CHRISTIE gave birth to a beautiful baby boy the day before hospitals stopped allowing visitors. She was lucky that both sets of grandparents had the opportunity to meet Henry. However, beyond that, friends and family didn't have the privilege of seeing the newest member of the family. These restrictions, although necessary, made for a more difficult start than expected.

Christie saw a beautiful Front Steps Project maternity picture of her friend on social media.

What a cool idea, Christie thought. She reached out to Susan and told her what was going on. It would be really special if Christie could get some family pictures with their newborn to announce him to all the friends and family who were not yet able to meet him.

The pictures, of course, were beautiful. However, the unexpected joy was not from the photos themselves.

The family had something to look forward to. Recently and very suddenly (and a little beyond her four-year-old comprehension), big sister Eloise had no daycare, no playtime with friends, and no park to look forward to. But for the photo shoot, she was able to choose her favourite outfit and get dressed up in something she enjoyed as if she were preparing to go to a birthday party or somewhere special.

After a week and a half postpartum, Christie found pleasure in doing her hair, putting on makeup, and wearing "real" clothes for the first time in a long time. Planning and coordinating the event gave the family something to anticipate, and they were all very excited.

A breath of positive energy permeated the house, not only in the preparation for the event but also after they received and shared their pictures.

"The most special thing for us was not just that we had these pictures, but we had this moment to celebrate and to be so proud of our family," Christie mentioned to her husband, Ryan, afterwards.

"You are right," he added. "Joy is about the people, not the photos."

APPARENTLY, SUSAN'S DESIRE TO BRING joy extended far beyond the beautiful representation of people—pixels on screen, exposure, and focus. It gave one family the gift of contentment for an entire week. And like the pictures, that memory will also last forever.

Susan Gaudet is the owner of Anita Marie Photography, a company named after her late mother. Susan believes that no matter where life takes you, a photo can always bring you back home. Check out her socials @AnitaMariePhotography.

Christie Stetson is a high school teacher in Prince Edward Island.

Photo credit: Anita Marie Photography

LAUNDRY LOVE LETTERS AND GROCERIES ARE NOT CANCELLED

By Susan Cruickshank

I COULD FEEL THE WEIGHT of fatigue as I stepped out of the shower. I hadn't emptied my bowels in over a week, and they were accustomed to moving daily. Standing on the bath mat with a bright pink towel wrapped around my torso, my wet hair dripping big droplets of what was now cold water on my shoulders and back, I looked straight ahead blankly. The idea of taking the squeegee to the shower's glass doors and then turning on the washing machine, already holding the clothes I had worn that day, seemed more than I could do as I ploddingly began to towel off.

The night's new bathing routine and small load of laundry were due to the COVID-19 pandemic. The extra measures were a conscious effort to minimize the risk of infection and its spread. News outlets were telling us to keep our distance, but it still wasn't clear to me if I could bring home coronavirus particles on my clothes or in my hair. I surmised that washing the things I had been wearing while out, immediately upon my return, and taking a shower were all good things. A pre-emptive effort to destroy any nefarious microbes that I had unwittingly carried back to the house on Indian River after a grocery errand. I was worried because I was staying with my friend's folks, and her mother had respiratory issues—a bull's eye symptom for this disease that was now attacking people's lungs.

I am a writer who pet- and house-sits, mostly in Ontario, in order to keep my expenses low while also giving me the time to write. I call myself a responsible nomad. Not having any family of my own, this vagabond lifestyle has allowed me to cobble together a small but meaningful life.

In my particular field of work, planning ahead is essential. I try to stay as close to my goal of back-to-back jobs as I can, but inevitably there are gaps, where my need for a home base is necessary. Peterborough has been the location of my base camp for years, but life has shifted, as it does, and what had worked well for so long now does not, and I have been required to look for a different middle step.

This was the case when I landed at my friend's parents' door on March 8, 2020.

I had another booking with a senior boxer named Bo that began on March 10, but I needed a place to stay in the two-day interim.

It was only two days.

My friend's parents live just outside of Peterborough in a sweet spot on the river, and so I made arrangements to nest with them while in the gap. But that was before the world began to shut down, my sit was cancelled, and everything stopped.

That was three weeks ago.

Don and Mary are good, kind people. Salt of the earth, generous to a fault, a devoutly religious couple who walk out their faith rather than just talk about it. But still, staying indefinitely, especially in a time of such apocalyptic stress, was, well, it was asking a lot.

But when I arrived, they welcomed me with open arms, demonstrating, by example, one of their Catholic faith's edicts, "to harbour the harbourless." And I was most certainly harbourless.

As news reports continued to spout grim facts and disheartening forecasts, I decided to drive into Peterborough the second week of my stay to do a blowout shop. One last swan song of grocery shopping before hunkering down for good. My friend's folks already had a full pantry of supplies, but I wanted to add another contribution before hanging up my car keys and becoming housebound, travelling no farther than the lonely country road outside their front door for long, solitary rambles.

It was a risk to take this trip. Auntie Mary already had trouble breathing. I was aware of the danger but reasoned that the number of cases would only continue to climb, and so it was better to go now rather than wait. I made my plan. I would shop later in the evening when in-store traffic was light. And when I returned to the house, I would immediately wash the clothes I had worn for my expedition and would shower and wash my hair.

I had done just that, and I could hear Auntie Mary in the kitchen putting the groceries away as I stood on the beige terry-cloth bath mat, still dripping as the shower's steam began to evaporate. Uncertainty and deep exhaustion remained in the last vapours of mist as they descended, me unmoving, sinking in like lotion.

The washer and dryer are also in the bathroom, and so after I finished towelling off and getting into my pyjamas, I turned on the machine. And then I shuffled down the hallway in my bedroom slippers to the kitchen. I wanted to ask Auntie if I could hang my damp things up in the morning as I was too tired to wait until the load of washing finished its cycle.

She said, "Of course, girl. You just go on to bed and we'll see you in the morning."

My bladder is not what it used to be, and so middle-of-the-night trips to the washroom are regular occurrences. That night I stumbled down the dimly lit hallway, a night light guiding my steps. My eyes squinted once inside the bathroom, adjusting to the brighter light, and then growing wide and incredulous as they took in what they saw. Hung neatly around the bathroom were all of my drying clothes. The generosity of such a small gesture reassured me, a constipated wayfarer standing in the stillness of the deepest night, that I was welcome in the storm and my innards could relax. My heart filled up to bursting, so touched by the thoughtful act that my eyes immediately spilled warm tears.

But it was when I went to the sink to wash my hands that I saw her note. It read:

Good Morning,
Sorry the Mother came out in me last night
& when it did I got mega energy.
What JOY I felt doing something for my little girl Susan.
God Bless,
Mom #2

23

How grateful I was for Auntie Mary's gesture of grace. I walked back to bed with such a feeling of peace and contentment. I knew everything was going to be okay; it already was.

Susan Cruickshank is a dual citizen who makes her home base in Indian River, Ontario, but spends part of her year living in Vermont's Green Mountains. She is growing her freelance writing— Vermont Magazine, The Sunlight Press, Positively Positive—*while chipping away at her first book, a memoir. You can find her on Facebook and Twitter: @LivingANewFuture*

MASS IS NOT CANCELLED

BY HEATHER DOWN WITH FR. PASSERO

WHEN THE BISHOP MADE THE decision that Catholic churches would no longer be open to the public and that mass would be celebrated in private because of the coronavirus, Father Rico Passero of St. Joseph Parish in Grimsby, Ontario, took this to prayer: "Lord, what are some ways I can keep our people connected to you and to our church?"

Later that day after finishing his prayer, Father Rico went back to the office to take care of some administrative duties, and he happened across an article on Facebook about a priest on the outskirts of Milan, Italy, named Father Giuseppe Corbari. Italy had been hit hard by COVID-19. When the churches in Italy went on lockdown mode, Father Giuseppe didn't want to celebrate mass staring at empty pews, so he sent out an electronic call to his people, asking them to send in selfies and photographs of themselves to be taped to the pews. He would then be able to look out and "see" his congregation when he celebrated mass.

I am going to do the same thing here at St. Joseph, Father Rico thought.

He approached the parish pastoral team—the staff—with the idea and was met with resounding support. The parish had a photo directory, so they began by printing the 450 photographs of the families who had participated in getting their pictures taken. But the parish consisted of 3,000 families, so Father Rico subsequently put out a request for other families, if they wished, to send in selfies.

Father Rico was a little apprehensive because some people might be sensitive about their pictures being printed. However, he couldn't have been more wrong. All the parishioners were eager to participate and thought this was a fantastic idea.

The pastoral team and Father Rico went around taping the printed photos on the pews, but not just on any random pew. They placed the picture where that family would normally worship on a weekend. His whole idea was to bring some hope to the people of St. Joseph because yes, they could watch Toronto mass online, but this was *their* parish; this was *their* community. He wanted them to stay connected with their local parish.

That was Father Rico's original intent. However, he felt that God was using this idea to bring great hope to more people, and this wasn't just about St. Joseph. He realized this was something any priest could do, and the idea blossomed into a beautiful way to keep people together.

Father Rico streamed Sunday mass on his Facebook account, the parish YouTube channel, and the church's website. In a perfect world, the congregation would be physically present. However, Father Rico believed this would help his parish remain spiritually connected and allow people to not feel abandoned.

Media agencies across the country interviewed Father Rico, and soon he was met with more requests from across the country. "Would you include our picture, too?"

The idea spread quickly, and friends on Facebook—from Europe and the United States—made this idea go global. Many priests started streaming mass online. Father Rico believes this was a great way to use technology to bring people closer to God during trying times. Instead of being drawn into fear, Father Rico believes we are called to be people of peace. Having a physical representation of his parishioners brought them comfort in a time when they needed it most.

Father Rico Passero is a priest in Southern Ontario, where he is Director of Vocations in the Diocese of St. Catharines.

GIVING BACK IS NOT CANCELLED

BY DAVE THOMAS WITH SRI SELVARASA

MORE, PLEASE . . . IS WHAT BEGINS to form in my mind as I listen to Sri's story develop.

"I know what it's like to be hungry. I know what it's like to be scared. I know what it's like to be hiding in bunkers with my brothers and sister, wondering how this might end. I know what it's like to be helped by others."

His narrative flows. He is clearly in the zone now. A chord within him has been struck by speaking of these prior experiences, and every fibre in his body is reverberating. I can feel it. A passion has been aroused and is propelling him forward.

"My country was in a civil war. My father got out first and went to Vancouver, where he worked in restaurants. The rest of us got out in 1989 and came to Toronto, where my dad had moved to start his own restaurant. I was ten years old when I came with my brothers—two younger, one older, and my eldest sister."

All four brothers now work in the restaurant, so it is truly a family business. Restaurants tend to come and go, but after twenty-five years Little India Restaurant is entrenched as a part of the Queen Street West area. The current public health lockdown has had an impact on the entire restaurant industry, and there is now no sit-down service here—the tables are empty. They still offer a takeout service. Before the pandemic, they used to serve about 130 or more people a day at the tables. I do some mental calculations and cringe.

A lady, probably in her fifties, walked in a couple of weeks ago. She was polite but with an aura of lack in her life. "I need to eat. I can't pay right now, but I promise I will pay later, when I can."

That, too, struck a chord. Sri prepared a meal-in-a-box arrangement and put it on the counter in front of her. "You don't need to pay," he said, clearly affected by the exchange.

Shortly after, Sri met with his brothers. They all know what it is like to be hungry, scared, and wondering how it might end. They quickly agreed that they want to help. They recognize this as a time of need, and that they can now be on the other side of the giving-and-receiving equation. He verbalizes to me his joy at being able to help.

Today, in the empty dining area, a table is dedicated to free meals, with two options: one vegetarian and the other a chicken-based dish. Guests can come in and take what they wish from this table with no questions asked. They can do this every day, and some do.

"We don't ask questions. We choose to respect people's dignity. I don't think people are abusing this arrangement." Clearly these brothers are aware of the physical needs of those they help, but they are also sensitive to the possibility of psychological fragility.

"It's not just us. Many folks are helping. A few days ago, three young people came in and asked for twenty meals, which we provided, and they distributed them to the street people in the area. People are stepping forward, coming together in many ways while keeping apart. For us, it's about showing love!"

Something is happening to me. I am lifted, inspired, awed, wanting to hug, cry, commend, exude something, kneel, pray, thank God—I don't know what's appropriate, but maybe the sense is more purely described in questions: "What resides at my core, what is compelled of me? And by whom, or what? Within me, yes, *me*, is there such a spirit?" I am used to hearing about humanity's ugly side—greed, envy, dishonesty, selfishness. But have I been misled, or have I been looking in the wrong places, or have I just been blind? I ask Sri: "Where did this desire in you come from?"

"I think to some extent we learned this from our father. He was always helping people, and we are still sending money to people back home. In the restaurant right now, we have various types of people taking the free meals—students, artists, people in mobility chairs, families with kids . . . We provide meals to three shelters when we can." He pauses slightly, and I think: *Can it be that we learn this heart, this compassion, this behaviour, this love, at least in part, by example? If so, have I improved my community by mine? Dare I examine my life?*

"We will do this as long as the budget allows, and we can get supplies. Some food supplies are harder to get right now. I used to pay \$15 or \$20 for a box of peppers that now costs us \$45," he says.

I tell Sri thank you for what he and his brothers are doing. Our chat has brought me to a point of not knowing what else to say or ask. I am afraid that my voice will crack if I don't stop here, so I do. I am affected in many ways, at different levels.

I think of a father leaving five children behind and coming to a strange country, alone. I think of five scared children clinging to each other in a war-torn homeland, without their father. I think of adult brothers sending money oversees to people they left behind. I think of their language, their cultural and religious heritage that they have adapted to a new environment.

And I imagine an immigration officer who looked at their applications some twenty-five years ago and stamped "Approved," and I can only think . . . *More, please . . . more people like these folks!*

Dave Thomas is a semi-retired lawyer living in downtown Oshawa with his wife, Sandra, where they enjoy interacting with inner-city residents, surroundings, and agencies.

Sri Selvarasa was born in Jaffna, Sri Lanka. He has three kids— two boys and a girl. He loves watching basketball and spending time in nature.

Photo credit: Nancie Wight

LEVITY IS NOT CANCELLED

BY HEATHER DOWN WITH NANCIE WIGHT

BEING INVOLVED WITH TECHNOLOGY, COMMUNICATION, and media was a reoccurring intersection in Nancie's life. This Montreal-area creative had a myriad of accomplishments and careers: completing one of the first master's degrees of multimedia in Canada (before anyone knew what multimedia was); performing stand-up comedy on the weekends while teaching at Concordia during the week; helping to pioneer the mobile content industry as an executive with a cutting-edge media company working with the likes of Disney, HBO, A&E, History Channel, and Deepak Chopra; and achieving the status of wildlife photographer.

Never did Nancie imagine that her past experience in the field of multimedia, mixed with her penchant toward humour and storytelling, would lead her to what happened next.

Occasionally, Nancie would animate her miniature schnauzer, Pluto, using an app, making it appear that the dog was talking. She would add funny commentary to make entertaining videos for her friends on Facebook—particularly for special occasions such as birthdays. She posted an end-of-year report at the conclusion of 2019, spoken from the perspective of her beloved thirteen-year-old "four-legged." Nancie rarely made public posts; however, her friends insisted she not take this post down and that she keep it public because they wanted to share Pluto's humour.

A couple of months afterwards, the pandemic hit Canada. Nancie came across a story about someone who was buying up a lot of toilet paper to resell at a profit on Amazon. Hoarding and price gouging was unfathomable. In fact, Nancie found it down-right annoying. *Really?* She thought. *Someone would do something like this?*

This set the wheels turning. Like most people, she was feeling concerned, overwhelmed, and in need of some levity. Physical dis-tancing was now in effect, and people were starting to feel isolated and on edge. It was time to create another Pluto video. Nancie started to rip on the crazy toilet paper issue, and the video evolved from there. It began:

> Hello Internets. It's Pluto here and I'm getting a feel-ing that there is a kind of crisis for the two-leggeds so I thought I could share some perspectives from the four-leggeds and maybe that could help you. So we like to just chill out at home, we curl up, we wander around, play with a tennis ball, there's lots that you can do. I heard there is a crisis with the toilet paper, which I don't understand. I mean, for cats, I understand because they like to play with it, but cats aren't that important. But for humans, what my mom does for me is she cuts the hair on my bum really, really, really short and the stuff comes straight out of me. There's no worry. It's all good . . .

The next morning Nancie woke up to hundreds of private messages and new friend requests. She was shocked. *Okay, I have to do something. I have to direct people to somewhere else because I can't do this.* Nancie decided that Pluto needed her own Facebook page, and she funnelled people to the newly created Pluto Living page, thinking it would be this little thing that could brighten a few people's day with a couple of videos.

However, Nancie couldn't be more mistaken. The video went viral, and Pluto almost broke the internet. She had officially become an influencer. Within two weeks, Pluto Living had over

170,000 followers from all corners of the world. One early private message in particular hit a chord: a lady from Rome was absolutely beside herself with anxiety. She mentioned she had been so stretched with worry and hadn't laughed in a couple of weeks. Pluto's video was such a relief, causing her to laugh until the tears streamed down her cheeks. She was so thankful for the release.

Nancie's inbox was flooded with similar messages—beautiful but overwhelming—and she had to set up an autoresponder. However, she continues to scan every message. Even though pictures of pets, heart emojis, and notes of encouragement were appreciated, Nancie wanted to be very careful not to miss messages from people struggling with their day-to-day lives, as well as nurses, doctors, and caregivers. Despite receiving hundreds of messages each day, she believed some of the correspondence needed to be addressed personally, especially from those working in front-line health care.

It was tiring, but Nancie continued to sift through all the messages because she felt it was her way to give back. One woman who was hearing impaired told Nancie she never thought she would see the day when she would try to lip read a talking dog! Nurses from incredible ICU teams reached out asking if they could do anything *for Nancie*, and some health care staff, after seeing a video of Pluto snoring, sent messages telling her to wake up so the group could watch her next video before hitting the front lines. When Pluto was featured on CBC's *The National*, one fan watched the news segment over and over in every time zone!

Nancie was not expecting to have touched so many people. It was a moment in time, all of it coming together in one place to bring joy in the darkness. But isn't that the best we can do—just be kind? The phenomenon is best summarized in the words of Pluto herself: "It's really important that you all be good to each other . . ."

Besides being Pluto's mom, Nancie Wight has been a wide variety of things including a stand-up comic and a wildlife photographer. You can follow her talking miniature schnauzer @plutoliving.

WEDDING STORIES ARE NOT CANCELLED

BY ROB DEKKER

WE HAD NO EXPECTATIONS FOR what would take place in ten days as we boarded our flight to Vancouver. We knew we had to be aware of our actions because of COVID-19. Before we sat in our seats, we wiped them down, head rest, arm rests, and the back of the seats in front of us. The one thing we were thankful for was that the virus must have caused some cancellations—the plane was only half full, and we had the luxury of not having a third person in our row. I had the sense that everyone on the flight was doing their best to restrain from coughing, blowing their nose, or doing anything that might raise the eyebrows of our fellow passengers.

Liz felt she had to go; no plans had been cancelled as of our flight time. She felt it would be unfortunate if the mother of the bride was not present for her daughter's biggest day of her life. We were going; there had been no demand from government not to travel within Canada. As we made the decision, we knew what to expect our time in Vancouver to be like. We had been watching the daily briefing with Dr. Bonnie Henry. We had become fans, watching how she calmly updated and advised British Columbians and Canadians on COVID-19. We made our decision to travel based on her instructions to BC residents—so there we were, 20,000 feet in the air going west.

Our trip to the Ottawa airport to leave for Vancouver was fast, and the airport was a lot less busy than we had seen it before, but we were not prepared for the scene when we arrived in Vancouver. The hustling airport was eerily quiet as we walked through to claim our baggage. Since international flights were being banned, YVR was a ghost town.

We had the pleasure of having dinner with groom Matt's mother and her partner. Both mothers were named Liz, but it was clear that beyond their name, they had much in common.

They both had a desire to see the wedding take place. They talked over dinner about the ceremony and how they could make sure everyone attending would stay safe. When dinner ended, there was still some doubt it could be pulled off. However, there was still optimism that Christa and Matt would be married by the end of the next weekend.

Throughout that first weekend, I watched events unfold. Through Saturday and Sunday, calls and texts were being received that elderly aunts and uncles would not be able to attend. Travel plans had been cancelled, but there was still hope. The big question was whether Briana, Liz's other daughter in Ontario, would travel. With her husband and two young daughters, the challenge was getting through the fear that they would not get back to Ontario, that somehow they would be spending fourteen days in isolation in BC—or worse yet, get back to Ontario and then find out they might spread the virus to others.

This was but just one conversation about the wedding. Many were also being held on Matt's side of the family. His brother, a first responder, had his young family live with his sister-in-law while he was working, all to protect them from the coronavirus.

Finally, the call was made, tears were flowing, and it seemed like the world was caving in. Plans made a year in advance were slipping away like the collapse of a mudslide that takes a house. The foundation is first affected—in this case it was family and friends not coming. Christa's BFF would not come, the hairdresser cancelled, but when Briana made the call that she could not come without her daughters and husband, it hit hard.

The foundation of the families not being able to properly gather for the events caused the whole wedding to crash down. It was at this moment everything else gave way. The virus had hit close to the resort outside of Whistler, where the wedding was to take place. Because of this, they agreed to offer full refunds to guests. Matt sent an email (Christa couldn't do it) to everyone invited. The wedding was cancelled. It would be rescheduled at the same place on a different date. Matt had been sending the emails about the wedding from the moment he proposed—they contained his humour and wit and made you laugh when you read them. This email was different. He tried, but he couldn't mask the sadness he and Christa felt in making this decision.

Travel bans were in place moving to and from the United States. Federal, provincial, and local health authorities were issuing stern warnings about physical distancing. We watched as across Canada, the number of infections increased, and businesses slowly shut down in their attempts to slow the spread and flatten the curve of the virus.

There was one saving grace in everything that was happening—the weather. It was amazing weather, sunny every day. This helped ease the pain of the decisions that were made. Matt and Christa started to find other things to do. The backyard needed work. This was a great time to trim the cedars, cut the grass, and get the garden in shape for the summer. It was a good escape from the reality of the day.

We visited with Matt's mom (Liz D) and Ian for tea in order to plan a new wedding.

The original plan had been for Christa's best friend, Kerri, to act as the officiant of the ceremony and then have a commissioner present to seal the deal. Matt's best friend from his youth, Bruce Arthur, was the best of the best. He, too, had been kept home and couldn't attend. A highly regarded sportswriter for the *Toronto Star*, he had been seconded to write COVID-19 stories.

Liz D and Ian's home became the place where the two moms turned into wedding planners. Christa and Matt were told not to worry—they would still be married. All Christa had to do was find a commissioner.

Over tea, plans were made to scout for a wedding location, marking the occasion with a simple but meaningful display for the wedding ceremony; enlist a family friend to take photos; and pitch the story of the wedding to the sportswriter.

There were simple and important criteria to be met for the wedding; it had to be near the water, a beach was preferable, and the ski hill where Christa and Matt had met should be in the backdrop. Locations were scouted. One was too windy, another was too dark, and another was likely to be busy when we needed it.

Matt used his social media network, at the insistence of Christa, to find a hairdresser. He scoffed but posted the question, asking if any of his friends knew of anyone who could do an updo. He stopped scoffing when an old friend agreed to do it. She had been a hairdresser but had stopped a few years back. I guess it's like riding a bike: you never forget.

Simple accessories were gathered: flowers, ribbon, and chalkboards. There would be champagne afterwards in Liz D and Ian's garden. This would be a safe-practices coronavirus wedding.

The commissioner hired for the original wedding could not perform their duties in Vancouver. Calls were made to local commissioners for the ceremony: they were busy—very busy. Decisions needed to be made over the phone, no personal meetings on such a tight timeline. Christa found the one who was a perfect fit for them, simply by voice alone. She was available; the noon wedding filled a hole in her schedule. She had two more weddings that day.

Everything was coming together as planned by the two moms. The weather seemed to be cooperating—the weather forecast for the day of the ceremony was improving as the week went along.

Saturday, the sun was shining, and clothes we had packed for the wedding were finally taken out of the suit bag. We'd dressed in jeans and T-shirts for a week; it was a nice feeling to get dressed up. Matt had gone for a bike ride in the morning, Christa was getting her hair done, Liz and I were cleaned up and wedding ready.

We arrived at Jericho Beach. Liz D and Ian arrived early and prepared the spot. As planned, Cypress Mountain was in the background, the snow cap visible. Crossed skis were set up at the "altar." Flowers were attached to the skis, and chalkboards with representations of Christa (on a bike) and Matt (on cross-country skis) were planted in the sand. A table was set to the side for the signing of the documents. It was only appropriate that the two Lizzes were official witnesses to the marriage. On the table was a photo of Matt's father, who had passed away a few years before.

He was watching, too. In true safe COVID-19 practices, Liz D brought the hand sanitizer and the disinfectant wipes.

A camera was set up to film the wedding, but without a proper mic, all you heard was the wind. Their vows when spoken carried into the air to become part of the beach forever. Briana, her husband, and her two girls watched via FaceTime with Christa's father, who also was unable to attend in person. Just like the video, it was a ceremony to see and not hear.

As Christa and Matt walked the aisle of warm sand, everyone else self-distanced themselves. Christa wore a beautiful spaghetti-strap gown with a faux fur shoulder wrap. She discarded her shoes and walked barefoot in the sand. Matt sported a blue suit, open-neck white shirt, and white runners.

A wide circle embraced the bride and groom. Gordo, Matt's uncle, rode his e-bike from Strathcona to Jericho Beach, a thirty-minute ride. Matt's brother and sister were there. Liz stood beside me; I had my arm around her as she watched her daughter get married.

A family friend photographed the wedding with a telephoto lens—getting the close-up in a time of being distant was never so easy. The group photo signified just how much the world had changed in only a few weeks. In a photo of the ten people who attended the wedding, only Christa and Matt embraced; the rest of us stayed in our six-foot bubbles.

We gathered afterwards in the garden of Liz D's home, its beautiful bamboo trees, vines, and spring flowers in bloom. The afternoon sun kept everyone warm from the breeze. Following a champagne toast, the two mothers gave speeches to eight people (originally intended for fifty). Liz made wraps for everyone for lunch, all in sandwich bags personally labelled. Liz D served cake, a miniature version of the cake that Christa had to cancel just the week before.

It took only a little gentle persuasion for the first dance to take place on a twenty-square-foot dance floor of interlocking brick. Just like everything else that happened on this day, it was only a small taste of what we'll see next year.

Matt's best man, Bruce—the *Toronto Star* writer—sent a link for the story of the wedding. It was a story of Christa and Matt, their friends, the two Lizzes, the story of a love that would not be denied. It was online Sunday night and would appear in print on Monday on the front page below the fold.

Monday we were at the airport for our 6:45 a.m. flight home; we were not even sure the flight would happen. We only believed it after we were safely in our seats. On our layover in Toronto, we picked up copies of the *Toronto Star*, one for Christa and Matt, one for Christa's dad, and one for Liz D.

The newspapers were to be a memory of the wedding and the week that was—not that we'll ever need it. Something beautiful happened: it was unexpected, and it was something we'll never forget.

Rob Dekker lives in downtown Ottawa where he has worked since 2016 as Director of Policy for a federal member of Parliament. Rob is an avid reader and writer who believes that communication strategies and the use of social media can be a force for social good and for business success. You can follow Rob on Twitter: @robertdekker or on Instagram: @rdekker1960 or read his blog: www.redheartbluesign.wordpress.com

DANCING IS NOT CANCELLED

By Heather Down with Jordan Lincez
and Gurdeep Pandher

ALTHOUGH BORN IN KAPUSKASKING, ONTARIO, Jordan spent most of his formative years in the Ottawa area. At the age of thirteen, he joined the cadets. At summer camp at Base Borden, in addition to experiencing his first real kiss and almost getting sent home for administering a haircut gone wrong, he learned to play the bagpipes.

After two years, Jordan quit cadets and lost access to the pipes. As an adult, life would take him to Japan to teach English as a second language, then to Vancouver to obtain his teaching degree. Teacher strikes without any light at the end of the tunnel caused Jordan to consider moving to the Yukon. He had visited there a few summers prior and had fallen in love with it.

Jordan taught at an elementary school in Whitehorse. The principal of the school was looking for a substitute piper for an assembly and somehow heard that Jordan used to play.

"Jordan," she broached the topic. "We really need someone to play the bagpipes at our upcoming ceremony. Do you think you could help us out?"

"Oh, I really don't know. I haven't played for twenty years."

"I would appreciate if you would consider it. We don't have any options."

Jordan visited the pipe major, Pat, at the local Midnight Sun Pipe Band, who managed to locate and dust off a set of pipes Jordan could use.

During the assembly, Jordan's debut rendition of "Amazing Grace" was . . . memorable. As he squeaked his way through his approximation of the song, his face turned red but not as red as the faces of the upper-grade students who were shaking with laughter. Even the entire front row of kindergarten children had covered their ears with their hands. Jordan had given new meaning to the phrase "sounds like strangling a cat."

Any possible hope that maybe Jordan's valiant effort was appreciated by someone—*anyone*—was completely eradicated when the kindergarten teacher mentioned, "Oh, my dear. Jordan, I forgot to tell the students there would be a loud instrument at the assembly. Three children had to change their pants afterwards."

Knowing his playing was the cause for three little kids to soil themselves, a deflated-but-not-defeated Jordan knew he needed more practice—and practise he did.

Jordan vastly improved and joined the Midnight Sun Pipe Band. He even travelled to Cape Breton to participate in piping workshops.

When a friend scooted off to New Zealand, and her cabin outside Whitehorse became available, Jordan jumped at the opportunity. Decompressing outside of town appealed to Jordan and, although there was no running water, these cabins had electricity—and propane for heat instead of wood. They were semi-rugged but somewhat luxurious for wilderness living.

GURDEEP PANDHER, A SIKH MAN from the Punjab, originally hailed from the small town of Siahar in India. In 2006 he came to Canada and made it his new home. After finishing up a job in Lloydminster, Saskatchewan, Gurdeep decided to do some travelling.

In his wanderings, he fell in love with the Yukon. He found that sharing his love for bhangra dancing, a traditional Punjabi folk dance, was a way to break down barriers. He started offering lessons just for fun.

In a matter of a couple of years, it morphed into more of a career. Gurdeep had collaborated with Whitehorse mayor Dan Curtis and shot a dance video. To his amazement, the video went viral. It had over a million hits virtually overnight.

This ignited a passion, and Gurdeep has since filmed dozens of bhangra videos with Canadians from various walks of life including hockey players, provincial government staff, Indigenous groups, and members of the Canadian Armed Forces.

Gurdeep lives in a little cabin outside Whitehorse. His neighbour, of course, is Jordan.

WHEN THE PANDEMIC HIT CANADA, Gurdeep had returned home from being in Vancouver. Because he had been out of province, he self-isolated. He emerged and saw his neighbour across the way.

"Hi, neighbour," he said, both men cognizant of keeping physical distancing. Although their cabins were close, they weren't at all close by urban standards—a good thirty paces remained between them.

"Hey," Jordan responded. "Good to see you."

"Good to see you, too." Gurdeep began. "I have an idea. I am wondering if you would be interested in a collaboration."

"Sure, go ahead."

"Well, I have switched to doing shorter, more impromptu videos for Twitter instead of the longer music videos I was doing on YouTube. They are only about a minute. People seem to be liking that," Gurdeep began.

"Oh, that's cool." Jordan reflected. "I can see people preferring the shorter format."

"Yes. These videos are spontaneous and happy. Would you be interested in playing the bagpipes while I bhangra dance? To show two neighbours being joyful, doing what we love during this crisis? And maybe spread some hope."

This did not seem like a strange request to Jordan at all. Gurdeep had long since discovered that the quick rhythm of Celtic reels often played on bagpipes worked well with the bhangra style of dancing. In fact, India has a rich military history with bagpipes, which were introduced to the country by the British in the nineteenth century.

"Yeah. I am totally down with that."

A few days later, Gurdeep texted Jordan: **Hey, did you want to shoot the video Saturday morning?**

Jordan responded: **Sure.**

Gurdeep's purpose for creating this video was threefold: first, he wanted to promote physical distancing during this time of crisis; second, he wanted to show that joy, passion, and human connection with neighbours were still possible; and third, he wanted to celebrate diversity.

On Saturday morning, Jordan made the short trek to his neighbour's yard, bagpipes in hand, to shoot their joyous one-minute Twitter video.

When you watch the video, it might at first seem an unexpected juxtaposition: a Punjabi Sikh bhangra dancing, complete with a turban and argyle sweater-vest two metres away from a man of Irish/European descent, sporting a kilt made of his family's tartan and wearing rubber boots while playing the bagpipes, all against the backdrop of the Yukon wilderness—the framed background decorated with an outhouse boasting a crescent moon on the door.

If at first the entire scene seems out of place for the wilds of northern Canada, the thought is only fleeting, because when you look closely and give it some thought, you realize absolutely nothing could be more Canadian than this.

Gurdeep Pandher teaches bhangra dancing in the Yukon. You can follow him on Twitter @GurdeepPandher.

Jordan Lincez is a teacher in Whitehorse, Yukon, and he enjoys playing the bagpipes in the Midnight Sun Pipe Band.

CHANGE IS NOT CANCELLED

BY ROB LEATHEN

THIS YEAR STARTED OUT JUST like 2019 did for me, full of anger with everybody and everything—and harbouring a collection of negative beliefs about the moral character of the collective society. I battle with post-traumatic stress. Along with the many symptoms of PTSD, like the aforementioned anger, come many cognitive distortions. I have a lot of distorted beliefs about others and society. I believe that most, but not all, people are untrustworthy. I also believe that most will only look out for themselves and will only do good when it suits their needs.

In many ways in the early days of the COVID-19 pandemic, society did not let me down in proving me correct. I knew that many of my negative beliefs originated from my cognitive distortions, and yet countless people kept confirming my beliefs. To me, society was behaving exactly the way I expected self-absorbed, selfish, uncaring, disrespectful people to behave—almost like they were acting out a real-life script for a post-apocalyptic movie. Who could ever forget seeing images of people hoarding toilet paper, stripping shelves bare in grocery stores, leaving nothing for the elderly and most vulnerable? Who could forget seeing that couple buying up all the hand sanitizer and Lysol wipes only to resell them at greatly marked-up prices in an effort to profit from the pandemic? Who could forget seeing people willfully ignoring official requests to practise social distancing and self-isolation? Hearing people complain about stores and businesses being closed and social events like plays, movies, and concerts being cancelled didn't surprise me. All my distorted beliefs about people were being validated day in and day out.

But things started to change. Slowly, ever so slowly, I noticed that the media weren't focusing on the downfall of society as much. Attention turned away from panicked consumers toward the virus itself. Numerous experts were providing their opinions, which in many cases were not necessarily aligned. The world is on the verge of a catastrophe of biblical proportions and these experts couldn't even agree. How could my beliefs possibly be wrong?

Things continued to change. Many people in real life and on social media made an effort to inject some humour into the situation. Humour-filled social media posts started exceeding the number of serious COVID-19 posts. They were funny—some were really bad—but some were really, *really* funny. I actually laughed at quite a few. I took note that at least in my small corner of the world, people were honestly trying to make each other laugh and provide an outlet for the stress everybody was feeling. Unlike plays, concerts, and large social gatherings that had been cancelled, humour was obviously not cancelled. It appeared to be alive and thriving. Perhaps not everybody was as bad as I believed. Perhaps there were people who genuinely cared for and had compassion for others.

To my amazement, things just kept changing. Politicians of all stripes and political colours started working together for something bigger than themselves or their own parties. They started working together for the greater good of us all. This challenged my world view because I had always thought politicians, by definition, were confrontational and selfish. I thought they only pursued their party's agenda—yet during this pandemic, they were completely connected and acting as one.

Then I saw capitalistic, profit-driven companies taking steps to stop the panic buying. Some set aside specific times for the elderly and most vulnerable to shop. In some cases, they waived delivery fees and took action to stop those in society who were selfishly trying to profit from the pandemic and fear. Some businesses showed ingenuity and willingly switched their production lines to start making highly sought-after hand sanitizer, with a focus on supplying those on the front lines of the pandemic battle. Was it possible that not all businesses were driven by their capitalistic agendas and actually did compassionately care about the social side of society? Could I have been wrong about some of these companies?

Change, yup, it's happening. Not so slowly now. Many in society have started to respect those who, before the pandemic, had professions that were looked down upon or taken for granted: cleaners, grocery store clerks, truck drivers, delivery drivers, gas station attendants, pharmacists, doctors, nurses, first responders. That did not align with some of my beliefs about others.

Change, it's happening; it definitely hasn't been cancelled. You know what else hasn't been cancelled throughout this entire pandemic situation? Personal growth—not just for me but for many. Maybe, just maybe, some of my strongly held negative beliefs were wrong. Maybe the world isn't full of selfish, self-absorbed, uncaring, disrespectful people lacking compassion for others. The COVID-19 pandemic has helped me rediscover that, and I believe it has brought out the good in so many. Goodness, compassion, kindness, resiliency, and the social connection of the people and businesses that make up society have not been cancelled because of COVID-19. They are alive and well, in spite of this pandemic.

You know what *has* been cancelled because of this pandemic? My loss of faith in the goodness of people and the society they are part of.

Rob Leathen is a vocal advocate for first responder mental health. He uses his lived experience with PTSD and depression to help educate others through public speaking, presentations, and writing. His deeply personal story includes an account of his own mental health journey, detailing the milestones, mistakes, lessons learned, and keys to his success.

COLOURING IS NOT CANCELLED

BY HEATHER DOWN WITH PATRICK HUNTER

ORIGINALLY FROM RED LAKE, PATRICK Hunter, a two-spirit Ojibway artist and graphic designer, moved to Toronto from Sault Ste. Marie in 2011 after completing his studies at Sault College. Until 2014 he only painted and made prints, but then he decided to turn his art into a business. He began creating digital artwork to go on mugs and apparel; Patrick Hunter Art and Design was born. Patrick made a name for himself in the corporate world through collaborations with RBC, BMO, Ernst & Young, Staples, CTV, and Global Affairs Canada, to name a few.

Over time, Patrick had created a library of his digital artwork. He realized that if he converted these pieces to outlines, they would make extraordinary colouring books. And that was the birth of his first colouring book project.

Patrick then became the artist in residence for the Prince's Trust, a Royal charity with the mandate of aiding in the restoration of Indigenous languages. They collaborated on a colouring/language activity book. Two books were created with the help of Nelson Publishing and were translated by First Nations University in Saskatchewan into Swampy Cree, Ojibwe, and Oji-Cree.

Initially, the books were for the charity Teach for Canada, and 3,000 books were sent out to remote fly-in First Nations communities in northwestern Ontario where Teach for Canada taught. As an ongoing resource, the colouring books were also available online.

Once the pandemic hit, Patrick thought, *If ever there is a moment in history where Canadians might have more time to colour, that time is now.* He decided to post the link to these resources on his social media so people could download and print the books for free.

People were instantly drawn to the beauty, artwork, and language lessons in both books: *Things to Colour from Mother Earth* and *Beautiful Words from Turtle Island.* To his surprise, Patrick's link has been shared thousands of times! Many across Canada—and beyond—were downloading and colouring his books.

Patrick was pleased that, through his artistic expression, he could share something for free that would not only offer stress relief to the person colouring but could help spread his Indigenous culture and language.

Patrick Hunter is a two-spirit Indigenous Woodland artist from Red Lake, Ontario. He lives in Toronto but travels often around Canada, inspiring the next generation of Woodland artists to create a business from their artwork.

Photo credit: Patrick Hunter

PEACE IS NOT CANCELLED

By Michelle Sertage

MONDAY, 9 A.M. I AM quietly making my way downstairs, being sure to not wake anyone. I peek into my dad's room to see him sleeping peacefully on his new hospital bed. I smile. For a long time, he was resistant to admitting the necessity of a bed with the characteristic supportive mattress, rails, and lifters. One day, when the pain of moving became too much to bear, he finally surrendered to the idea. The bed was delivered the next day. Dad is happier, and we no longer have to spend the morning hours in reciprocated frustration, trying to get him into a seated position. We are *all* resting better.

I bring my memory back to a couple of weeks earlier, to a time when he could get up by himself. When he could dress, wash his hands, and even make it from his bedroom to the couch without support. So much has happened in so little time; I can barely remember these moments. Walking freely turned into needing a walker, then a wheelchair. Moving on his own turned into needing us with him for every step. His condition has been changing so rapidly, I can barely keep up. But his health isn't the only thing that has shifted dramatically in the past weeks.

It has been three weeks since I last served a customer at my job. Three weeks since I last left the house without the thought of making sure I touch as few surfaces as possible and to keep at least six feet of distance between me and every other person who crosses my path. The country—rather, the world—has been on lockdown mode ever since the coronavirus became a widespread, panic-inducing pandemic. In the past three weeks, I have seen what fear does to a society: from everyday people gathering apocalypse-sized stocks of non-perishables, to news channels and politicians shaming entire countries and spreading negativity. I have seen friends and family slip into patterns of depression and anxiety, fuelled by the lack of purpose they feel from not getting as much done in one day as possible. This is unprecedented, and it is scary. But the last three weeks have also given us a gift more beautiful than the fear it has also triggered.

My dad was diagnosed with stage IV lung cancer two years ago. It was a hard pill to swallow at the time, yes. But he was still being himself, and so the gravity of the situation hadn't yet pulled me out of the clouds and down to earth. I couldn't accept what was going on internally when the external representation of him was still as it had always been. I guess you could say I was in denial. As the months progressed and my dad went through different treatment regimens, reality started to take hold. My siblings and I started to accept our dad's declining health as the new normal, but it wasn't until just after the new year, only a few months ago, that we began to accept our new roles as his caregivers.

At first, being a caregiver wasn't overly taxing. We had to make sure his clothes were clean and that he had healthy food to eat. Of course, that quickly changed. With all of us in full-time jobs, it became more and more difficult to balance our new positions at home with our positions in our workplaces. Exhaustion and overwhelm quickly took centre stage, and it was hard to keep up with all of our duties inside and outside our home. Not only were we not able to give Dad the physical care he desperately needed, we also weren't able to be the emotional support his soul craved. As our proverbial cups dried up, and there wasn't much left in us to give, we heard the news of the stay-at-home order, with all non-essential businesses being forced to close. Work was cancelled, and all of a sudden, the weight we were feeling lifted. Air entered and filled our lungs, for what felt like the first time in months. We were finally able to breathe again.

For my family, this virus has gifted us the time we needed to spend with our dad in what could be his final months. The gift of permission to rest: filling up our own cups, so we are able to support him and each other as we grieve what was and anticipate what is to come. It is scary. Uncomfortable. But most of all, it is a beautiful reminder of what is truly important. For many in the world, this is a time in which fear and eventual grief will overtake reality. There are many things to grieve, but the overarching loss is the loss of the way things once were. Change, as my family has come to realize, is inevitable, challenging, and necessary. It helps us re-evaluate our priorities, to make room for what we will hold close to our hearts at the end of the day. As devastating as both this pandemic and the loss of our father will be, these moments help us appreciate life fully, for everything it has to offer.

I lay Dad's medication on his bedside table for him to have when he wakes up. I don't want to wake him quite yet; he looks too peaceful. I walk back up the stairs and grab my mug of tea. I open the front door and sit on the front step, taking in the day. All the driveways are full of cars and to my left, the neighbours' kids are playing outside, enjoying the early morning sun. I wave and then sit back, closing my eyes. The sunshine cascades over my skin, and I soak in its warmth. My lips curve upward as a smile blooms across my face. I breathe in this moment, deeply.

I, too, finally, am at peace.

Author's note: Two weeks after I wrote this story, on April 19, 2020, my dad passed away peacefully at home. No hospitals, ambulances, or chaos. Just him and his children, together for the last time, as he took his final breath. We will miss him greatly; and at the same time, we are all so grateful for the opportunity to have been home with him in his final weeks. Yes, the grieving landscape looks a lot different in the time of COVID-19. No funeral, no visitation, no friends or family around. But as we have navigated this new normal over the past months, we have learned to accept and work with what is. It isn't easy, and grief is a battle we are all facing, collectively, amidst the current social climate. Maybe the pain feels unbearable, and maybe meaning won't come for years. For me, I have faith in my heart that a greater teaching will surface after the suffering, and this is what will make the devastation easier to hold. In the meantime, we can take some deep breaths and be grateful knowing that, amidst the chaos, we have another day to experience the beauty of the world.

Michelle Sertage is a twenty-four-year-old yoga teacher with a passion for holistic health and healing. She loves travelling but is a homebody at heart. She is spending her quarantine days resting and regenerating for the adventures that lie ahead. Find her on Instagram @artofholisticliving.

GIRL GUIDE COOKIES ARE NOT CANCELLED

By Heather Down with Heather Mesher-Brown

HEATHER MESHER-BROWN CURRENTLY LIVES IN Happy Valley-Goose Bay. Although born there, life had taken her to the Northwest Territories, Nova Scotia, and Switzerland.

This deputy provincial commissioner of Newfoundland and Labrador Girl Guides was currently facing a dilemma. Heather was in charge of ordering the cookies for the spring drive. Every year, the cookies had to be ordered by the mid-fall deadline, and the size of the order was dependent on how many girls they had in the program that particular year.

Having no inclination that the world would be heading into a pandemic, Heather went ahead and ordered 360 cases of their bestselling signature cookies in October 2019. They had decided to set the bar high. They figured they could do it: they had a lot of girls in the program and decided to go all out.

In March, Heather received a phone call. "We are not sure where your cookies are in transit or if you are even going to get them. The national office is working on a strategy to help you sell them because we realize you can't go in the stores and set up a table or allow the girls to go door-to-door, selling to friends and relatives."

Heather was comforted that there was a plan in the works but honestly didn't know if the cookies would make their way to Happy Valley-Goose Bay.

After a couple of days, Heather received another phone call from a shipping company from Quebec. "Can we deliver?" they asked.

Heather wasn't sure if she should accept the shipment, but she was even more concerned about where the cookies might end up if she didn't.

"Sure. Deliver them to my house," she said.

Heather called her friend. "Hey, listen. The cookies are here now at my house. I'm going to offload from the truck. I'll store them in the meantime, but we will have to figure out what we're going to do."

Heather's house was overrun with cases of cookies. She posted on Facebook that if anybody in town wanted to purchase some cookies, they could send her an e-Transfer and she would drop them off on their doorstep.

Through hard work, Heather managed to move sixty cases, and some other guides sold another thirty or so during a six-day span.

This is tough, Heather thought. It was nearly impossible to sell cookies when you need to remain six feet apart. She knew this wasn't ideal, but what else could she do?

While surfing Facebook, Heather saw that the local Co-op grocery store was asking for boxes for deliveries to put groceries in because their community had a plastic bag ban. Heather messaged someone she knew on the Terrington Co-op board: I am selling these Girl Guide cookies from my house and the cases have handles. If the Co-op wants the empty cookie cases for groceries, you are welcome to them.

Heather's contact messaged back: I think the Co-op is going to buy eight cases of cookies, but I'll let you know. I'll call you in about an hour or so.

"Hi, Heather," her friend said when she called. "We are unable to use the empty case boxes for groceries due to health and safety

58

concerns. However, I have some good news. The Co-op is going to buy all the cookies."

"*All* of them? There are 3,168 boxes left."

"Yep, they want them all."

Heather started crying—they were tears of joy . . . and relief.

The Co-op purchased the cookies to resell at their store, but they also handed some out to essential workers in the community, dropping boxes off at the hospital, the police station, the fire hall, and the military police.

It struck Heather that it just shows how everybody bands together to help out. Her offer to donate the cookie cases didn't work out, but the Co-op reciprocated the kindness, filling in the gaps where needs could be met.

Heather Mesher-Brown has been a member of Girl Guides of Canada since 1994 and has volunteered with the organization in many roles. As an Indigenous woman, she has long-standing ties to Labrador and maintains connections to her Inuit ancestry and culture. When she's not volunteering with Girl Guides, Heather works in administration and enjoys spending time with her small family.

HOPE IS NOT CANCELLED

By Courtney Taylor

My THREE-MONTH-OLD DAUGHTER IS CURRENTLY asleep on my chest. This has been her favourite spot since she was born on January 9, 2020. She loves to be on her tummy, snuggled into the warm embrace and heartbeat of someone. Lately, however, that someone has been me 24/7.

In the first eight weeks of her life, she enjoyed this close and loving spot on many others—her village, which is how I have referred to them since before she was even born.

As a single thirty-something, after more than much thought and consideration, I decided to have a child on my own. I am what has been coined an SMBC—a single mom by choice. We are a group with more members than you probably realize; women whose biological clocks kept sounding, no matter how many times we tried to hit the snooze button. Thanks to the miracles of science and the willingness of men to share their required specimen, single women who desire motherhood can turn that dream into a reality.

I was lucky; I became pregnant last spring after only my second attempt through intrauterine insemination. Then my luck continued with a pregnancy where I endured nothing worse than some headaches and mostly manageable fatigue.

With plans to raise a baby without a partner, my luck also includes a village that's more the size of a city.

As someone who has always wanted to be a mother, and simply always assumed I would be, I spent years being an auntie to many, both by blood relation and by nothing more than pure love and friendship. Is there anything more, anyway?

My multiple circles of friends and family carried more excitement over the prospect of my impending motherhood than even I. Perhaps theirs was magnified by their collective sum, whereas mine was held only by me, in the sum of one. Regardless of the logic or mathematics, there were indeed many times throughout my pregnancy when many were more joyous and anticipatory than I was. Perhaps it was my own lifelong anxiety subconsciously protecting myself by putting a limit on overt excitement in the face of possible disappointment or tragedy; maybe it was as simple as the fact that they weren't being awoken three times a night to empty an increasingly compressed bladder; or, most likely, it was that they were quite simply jump up and down, over the moon happy for me—and indeed for themselves, looking forward not just to newborn baby snuggles but also to bearing witness to my transformation into a mother, *finally*! And I, though without a partner, had an army of people who couldn't wait to be aunties and uncles, grandmas and grandpas, and watch my baby grow up.

Watch my baby grow up.

Watching is, sadly, all any of them are able to do these days.

It's been almost a month since any of my daughter's "framily" members held her, or took a long inhale of her sweet-smelling baby head, or conversed with her in coos.

Thanks to the unprecedented global pandemic of COVID-19, my front door, which was revolving with visitors for the first eight weeks of her life, is now closed.

Lockdown. Quarantine. Isolation. Distancing. These are not welcome words to a new mom navigating the unfamiliar waters of life with a baby. They are the complete opposite of what I want, and what I crave.

Since before I was even inseminated, I've been travelling this road with my very involved village. They knew when I was considering this path, they knew when I decided to take it, and they knew I was expecting much earlier than the deemed safe three-month mark.

Now that my daughter is here, my village is on the outside looking in, figuratively and literally, for those few aunties who have stood outside my window to peek at her in person.

I know how these aunties and grandmas and others are missing their visits. How they (and I) can't wait for the days to come again when they can visit and cradle a content and cuddly little one. It is heartbreaking to me that I'm unable to share these fleeting once-in-a-lifetime moments with them all. The same moments so many of them lovingly shared of their own children with me.

I imagine the worst: that this isolation will continue for some time and my daughter's milestones will be met with only my memory to recall them.

I never intended to live this experience alone, even though I am without a partner.

And I don't intend to even now.

The silver lining of a pandemic-induced lockdown in the year 2020 is the technology that accompanies it. Though nothing can replace human contact, or the shared warmth of a hug or laughter echoing off the same four walls, we have the next best thing. We can still talk to one another, and we can still see one another, via photos and videos.

Photos.

I've always loved pictures. Taking them, printing them, framing them. They adorn the walls and shelves in practically every room in my home. Leaving them in virtual folders and clouds, seen only on a screen, has never sufficed for me. But it suffices for sharing.

On St. Patrick's Day, I dressed my daughter in an appropriately themed onesie, took photos, then shared them with my friends and followers online.

It made people smile. Her cherub mouth was turned up in a cheeky one of her own, the dimple that was passed down from her donor visible on her right cheek.

The following day she was dressed in too cute clothing, so I took another photo and posted it as well. The likes abounded. In the face of a new uncertainty and a worldwide fear, her sweet baby face was a bright spot.

So I continued to take a photo and post it every day. It gave me something to look forward to in a time when the calendar didn't count, when events that had been planned were cancelled just as fast.

Every day has brought the same thing: staying home. I sleep, I eat more than necessary, I nurse her, and I watch too much news.

In the repetition of every un-new new day, I found it fun to dress my baby girl, do a mini photo shoot, and then select the best shot to share.

In it others found fun, too. They shared that it brought them joy; they looked forward to it every day. They waited for her picture to appear on their newsfeed. In the barrage of bad news, in a bombardment of anxiety and worry, my baby's smile was a bright spot. Some told me that in all the doom and gloom of the daily death counts, her toothless, gummy grin was a ray of sunshine.

So the photos continue every day. It's become a daily ritual—for me, and for all who are currently loving her from afar.

Her villagers, whom I so miss sharing a tea and a couch (and maybe even a diaper change!) with, can continue to be a part of her life, and mine, in a time when we may sometimes feel like a part of nothing but our furnishings.

There are certain things that no distance or isolation can put a stop to: connection, history, love, friendship, hope.

Although we may be forced to cancel every shared event, to cancel all close contact with our people, our framily, our villages, we will not cancel our love for each other. We will not cancel our anticipation of time we may enjoy together again. We will not cancel better days when the light at the end of this pandemic tunnel starts to shine. We will not cancel what each of these things hold in common: hope. We will not, cannot, must never cancel hope.

How appropriate it should be that I named my daughter exactly that—Hope.

How lucky I am to share it daily.

Some Facebook Comments About #DailyHope

She makes me smile every post! Thanks.
– Betty Hoseman

A daily Ray of Hope is like sunshine to our hearts.
– Michele Sparling

She's sunshine on a cloudy day.
– Jean White

In these trying times, her smile lightens our day.
– Michael Lasitz

You are the sunshine of 2020 Hope. These pictures make my day.
– Barb Roberts

She truly makes my heart happy every day I see her pictures.
– Suzi Spelic

This little lovie makes my day every. single. day.
– Miriam Kemppainen

Every day I wake up and ask myself "How is Hope handling this world we are in?" And then when I see how Hope is making out, I know it's all going to be okay.
– Charlie Angus

Such an adorable distraction from the rest of the world!
– Laurie Gordon

Yaaaay, my Hope fix for the day. Love her.
– Donna Baldeo

Courtney Taylor was born and raised in the east end of Toronto, where she currently resides with her daughter, Hope, and her dog, Tucker. She is a proud mental health advocate and an avid reader, and she loves to cook. She was baking bread before it was "COVID cool."

Photo credit: Courtney Taylor

CHILDREN'S ART PROJECTS ARE NOT CANCELLED

BY SONYA ANDERSON

EIGHT-YEAR-OLD SCARLETT O'NEILL AND HER four-year-old brother, Easton, had no idea what a big impact the hearts they had carefully crafted and taped to their front door would have on their neighbours and all who walked by their house.

"I wanted to make people smile," said Scarlett. "It makes me happy to see my neighbours smile at my art."

Their mom, Carina, saw a heart art project on Facebook and thought it would be a fun activity she could do with her children while they were staying home as part of the effort to prevent the spread of COVID-19. She said now her children love to look out the window and see the joy their hearts bring to other people walking by.

Their hearts got noticed, and one neighbour posted a picture of their beautifully decorated door to her Neighbourhood Watch group and encouraged other children to share their art creations with the neighbourhood.

What followed has been an outpouring of love and beautiful pictures for young and old to enjoy as they leisurely stroll through the streets of their community. From instructional directives like "Wash Your Hands" and "Keep Six Feet Apart" to messages of thanks for our health care workers, this street art project spread quickly through the neighbourhood.

Some houses have used up every inch of window space for their children's messages and pictures, while chalk murals adorn the sidewalks with a beauty that even outshines the glory of the emerging spring flowers. And when it rains, the young artisans see it as a blank canvas that begs for another creation.

Eighty-six-year-old Eva Pizziol, who has been pushing her walker around the block every day since the snow melted, finds the artwork very uplifting and loves the efforts of the children who create these masterpieces. "I stop and read every message. They're so inspiring. I'm really touched that they're doing this so that we can all enjoy it."

Art's unique ability to arouse deep emotions in both the creator and the observer is what makes it especially therapeutic during challenging times. According to the Hospital for Sick Children, "Art is a natural language for children. It can help them make sense of and express their thoughts and feelings and improve coping."

Carina O'Neill feels that the art her children have created during this pandemic has been a way for her to strike a balance between teaching her children about the virus and the need for them to properly wash their hands and be safe, without traumatizing them in the process. Their hearts art project has allowed her children to focus their efforts on bringing joy to their neighbourhood instead of spending time focusing on their own anxieties.

Since decorating their front door, her children have started a flower garden project on the adjacent window that will eventually have a beautiful rainbow across its sky. And Scarlett has begun decorating the windows in her bedroom at the back of the house for her backyard neighbours to see. She's made a colourful message for them that reads, "We're all in this together."

It makes you realize that the simplicity of childhood wisdom is sometimes the best comfort for the soul.

Sonya Anderson is a freelance writer, a children's book author, and the owner of Sizzle and Sim, a multimedia production company through which she authors and publishes books and facilitates workshops aimed at encouraging school-aged children to write and publish their own stories. Her passion is writing heartwarming tales that help children and their families solve real-world challenges. When she's not writing, you can often find her travelling around the world with her pilot husband and globe-trotting kids.

KAYAKING IS NOT CANCELLED

By Teresa Hedley

I AM FLOATING. FEATHER-LIKE, SUSPENDED on the surface, I am still. Observing. Looking down, around, up, I am wrapped in nature. I am free. It can't get me here is the way I see it, and I hear that echoed around me.

We're safe out here!

Couples clinking wine glasses call out from sailboats. Families building driftwood forts nod from the shore. A guy in a homemade plywood rowboat raises a red oar. Fellow kayakers glide by and tip a paddle as they dip, purposefully, peacefully. Kiteboarders haul in their sails and enjoy a brew on shore, evenly spaced, visible at a distance by their sails, bright blue and neon green and outrageous orange in the slanting afternoon sun. A paddleboarder passes at a distance, head held high, scanning the inky swells, not lost at sea, but found here. We all are. We seek the sea for solace, for calm, for protection, for distraction, for rejuvenation, but mostly, for escape.

COVID-19 can't get us out here. I hear it again and again. In this, we are one.

As I float and bob and drift, my mind does likewise, drifting, floating, and at times bobbing, bouncing up and down, back and forth, reconciling how at a distance the world has changed, flipped, become unrecognizable.

And yet here, up close, hovering on the surface, nothing changes: blue herons continue to strike poses, steadfast stalkers poised to poke and pierce; eagles soar, elegant and fierce, eyes on the water, yellow talons extended like gnarly landing gear; seals pop up around us, curious, earnest, playful, hungry and big-eyed; sea lions bellow farther out, tracking herring, hungry hunters; farther still, plumes of vapour bisect the shoreline and we spy them, blasting, surfacing, shiny and black, the final link in the Pacific food chain: orcas.

It happens every spring, this chain, this chase—pandemic or not. The herring, the seals, the sea lions, the eagles, and the orcas are not aware of the drama unfolding on shore. They do their thing, oblivious, continuous. Life goes on out at sea.

And that's why we seek it, this nature-nurture: in nature, we trust. We seek its rhythm. Life as usual. Normalcy. Calm amid chaos. We seek to escape, to float, to observe, to be wrapped up, to be delighted, to savour, and to be safe. Here on the west coast, we seek the sea in droves, each of us in our craft of choice. Ours is the kayak.

Kayaking is not cancelled. Out we go.

Although we often paddle a predictable path, no two outings are alike. With the tide and in time, the ocean leaves us gifts. It tells us stories. We need to be vigilant observers, open to noticing. And we are. We do.

But first, the path and the process.

We live on a bluff over the ocean, two roads up, so we carry our kayaks downhill to the shore. That's step one. In front of us is an intriguing landform, perfect for exploration: a spit of land extending out into the harbour, a bit like a dogleg with canine toes splayed at the end.

But the way I usually describe it is more like an anatomical command: extend your left arm out in front of you, bend thirty degrees, and your arm becomes this spit of land. On your shoulder sits our house.

Your upper arm is the causeway, with beaches on either side. The outside is rougher open ocean. That shore is dotted with fire rings and strewn with driftwood and logs, perfect for fort-building. The inside is sandy, protected, good for kayakers, and in stormy weather, for kiteboarding enthusiasts.

Now, travel down to your forearm, beyond where the bend is. This portion is a military cadet camp, home to an international crew of eager cadets each summer.

At the very tip of your arm and this spit of land are your fingers and three bays: the gaps between your fingers. We call these quiet coves—from index finger to pinky—Heron Bay, Marina Bay, and Totem Bay. Each is home to its namesake.

Bigger picture, over your shoulder to the left rest the mainland mountains, distant and craggy, like the snaggle-toothed peaks beyond Seuss's Whoville, whimsically pointy and suggestively sinister, snow-capped, menacing. To the right and in front lies the island mountain range, closer and pleasingly smooth, *Sound of Music*-like, familiar and accessible. The jewel is the glacier, sleek and white, like a mammoth mother Persian curled up amid her litter.

That's the backdrop, your arm and hand, submerged in the sea, framed by mountains far and near. On we go.

We ease our kayaks into the edge of the bay, across from your hand. And then we do what we always do: we paddle across the stretch of water, heading for your forearm and a collection of shipwrecks. That's what I call them, but in fact, they are two rotting and abandoned homemade boats, washed up on shore. I prefer to think of them as heroic, so I call them shipwrecks.

"Meet you at the shipwrecks!" I call out to my son and husband, and off I go.

And this is where the story takes a turn and becomes a choose your own adventure odyssey (in my mind). I have choices, and although they have been curtailed and clipped on land, out on the ocean I am in control. Here in my kayak, I am free to choose. I slow my strokes and I hover. I bob. I imitate.

For what has happened is this: I've entered a jelly cloud, a patch of water filled with pulsing, translucent jellyfish, floating, pumping, rhythmic and beckoning. I slow down and then stop, still, watching, floating as they do.

Soon there are dozens. Hundreds? I stare down at them, an admirer of their delicate perfection: discs, feathery yet resilient, worker bees pumping, filtering and yet synchronized and sophisticated, simple and systematic. They become a ballet, and from my boat, I their admirer. The pulsing is calming, eloquent. Eventually I paddle on. This journey unfolds.

I reach the shipwrecks. The larger of the two is my favourite because it's a classic homemade, tubby-looking boat, a chipped and worn bath toy, resting on the shore at a three-quarter angle, resigned, recently pepped up with graffiti art. It looks like a rainbow Bob Marley from where I sit. *Isn't retirement grand?* That's what this boat says to me. I smile up at it, bleached and beached there, warm and tattooed in the gold late-day sun.

My son Erik catches up. We hover close to shore and wait for hubby and dad, Frank, to catch up, too. Neither of us speaks; we are both locked on to the ocean floor below us, magnified, like peering into an aquarium touch pool: broken bits of algae-covered oyster and clam shells; barnacles, grey and persistent, adhere to everything that does not move; and sea grass, moss green and mauve, sways gently to the rhythm of our crafts. Over there . . . a shard of glass, bottle-brown. Beer? A beach party?

"I love this, floating here . . ." I say to Erik. "It's like a Disney water ride where you don't have to do anything but sit and look."

He nods at me, unspeaking. In leaving the land behind, we put that life on hold: the headlines, the hand sanitizer, the alarming numbers, the predictions, the tragedy. Here we can float, detox, reset, rejoice.

Hovering on two feet of clear Pacific water, we have morphed into ride-goers, something between Disney's Pirates of the Caribbean and It's a Small World. We become observers in blue-and-white boats, mechanized by the current as it sweeps us parallel to the shore. We are drifting toward your thumb. Goodbye shipwrecks and touch pool. Goodbye wrist. On we go.

Heron Bay. This indent is the smallest and most unremarkable of the three bays, and yet it is here I notice most. Flanked by straw-like shore grass, Heron Bay is shallow and deserted, except for the pair of herons we once observed here, stoic, statue-like hunters. *Have the patience to do nothing* came to mind that day, and here, I do exactly that. Closing my eyes and lifting my face to the sun, I pause and listen. Eyesight eliminated, my hearing becomes masterful. There is much to take in.

What I notice most is the sound of water: the swells as they stroke the shore; the pleasing swish and slosh of Erik's and Frank's paddles exploring the bay; a sudden gush of rhythmic waves as they round the bend and smack sand. I do not see them, but I imagine them evenly spaced, like musical staff lines, bending and breaking as they collide with the shore. I hear the occasional gull, the rusty-clothesline screech of a distant eagle, the purr of a small plane. A Cessna?

Marina Bay is next. It's the largest and is home to a collection of boats belonging to the cadet camp. Over here, a line of faded sailboats, dressed down, resting and awaiting a new rotation of cadets. Over there, larger boats, pleasure craft. I discover, with a smile, song boats, love boats, and kids' boats.

Among the sonorous is one called *Against the Wind*. Bob Seger, soulful, reflective, downloads within: "I'm older now but still runnin' against the wind . . ." Another is *Summer Breeze*. The wind abates; the soundtrack shifts. "Summer breeze . . . makes me feel fine . . . blowing through the jasmine in my mind . . ." Ah, yes. Seals and Crofts.

The love boats are next. Three: *Magnetic Attraction, Goodnight Irene*, and *G. Louise*! And over there, the playful kids' boats, whimsical and light: *Oz* and *Peter Duck*. I need to see these names, all of them, a reminder that lightness and love are alive and well.

Totem Bay. We're almost there, to the tip of the spit, to your baby finger. But first, a wide but shallow bay where a single, stout, freshly painted totem pole resides and presides. The effect is spiritual. Maybe for this reason, I find myself reflecting. It is here I paddle and make sense of uncertainty. It is here I float and squint at the surface of the ocean, sparkly, dazzling in the afternoon light. It is here I process change. Erik paddles up beside me.

"This is my skating in circles," he says quietly, and I know exactly what he means. He is referring to our backyard skating rink in Ottawa, and how we used to skate in loops. Loops helped us to think, to understand, to process.

The three of us paddle together now, and exiting Totem Bay, we reach the sandy tip of the spit, deserted and exotic, for here stand two quirky driftwood shelters, makeshift and yet permanent. They have been here for as long as I can remember. What are they? Cadet projects? Survival huts? Equal parts creativity and random piecemeal construction, these unusual shelters offer a break from the summer sun. There are also two small driftwood totems jutting from the sand not far from the larger hut. Carved, grimacing faces give the beach a Polynesian feel. Exotic. Tropical.

But it is not to shore I paddle on this day. I head out toward the sailboats anchored in front, and as I glide by, I hear them, voices tucked inside or cast on deck, sound bites as I pass: "COVID-19" and "pandemic" and "death toll" and "Italy." The conversations merge, converge. Processing, endless processing.

And then something unexpected happens. I call out to the fellow on the white sailboat. He is sipping beer from a Mason jar. "Did you see that, just now, the blowholes out there? Orcas!"

I am bursting to speak, to mix and mingle . . . to make random connections with perfect strangers. To make up for lost time. To fill my chit-chat quota. I can out here; it's safe. And to my surprise, I find myself paddling from boat to boat, calling out, feeling talkative and a lot like my grandfather, Jack, rejoicing in what is hard to do on shore: connect.

A fishing boat passes, and we wait for it, the cascade of waves that will surely come our way. They do, soft, even swells that lift and buoy us. It feels like a haiku out here.

And that COVID-19 can't touch us.

Leaving your hand for open water, we head back toward your shoulder, for home. Reality.

I never knew what I liked so much about kayaking until now. Strangely, it took a pandemic to offer clarity. I return refreshed and reset. Ready.

The float has been heavenly.

Teresa Hedley is the parent of three young adults, one of whom, Erik, has autism. She is also an educator, an author, and a curriculum designer. As a teacher-trainer, Teresa taught English in Canada, Japan, Greece, Spain, and Germany. Her memoir, What's Not Allowed? A Family Journey with Autism, *is available on Chapters Indigo and will be released in October 2020. She and her family live and play on Vancouver Island.*

ROADSIDE ASSISTANCE IS NOT CANCELLED

BY HEATHER DOWN WITH ANDREA LOGAN

MERE MINUTES FROM HER HOME, Andrea simultaneously noticed the early morning lineup outside the local grocery store and the bumpiness of the road. She was on her way to the Hospital for Sick Children, where she worked in the Emergency Department some weekends when she wasn't straddling her full-time job as a pediatric nurse practitioner at Barrie's Royal Victoria Regional Health Centre and Orillia's Soldiers' Memorial Hospital. *This is really strange. I don't remember the road being this uneven,* she thought as this single mom chatted hands-free with her son, Colby.

Something was amiss. If she had a flat tire, wouldn't someone in that lineup try to flag her down? She needed to check. "Hey, I am going to have to let you go, bud. Mommy is going to have to call you back. I think there is something wrong with my tire. I need to have a look."

Andrea hung up and found a spot to safely pull over. *Oh, darn.* Surveying the damage, she couldn't help but say aloud, "I have a very flat tire and a bent rim. This is not good . . . not good. I am supposed to be at work for 10 a.m."

Andrea hadn't been at SickKids for a couple of weeks, so she had left her house with plenty of time to spare for the journey that usually took her just under an hour. It wasn't quite 8:15 a.m. With a flat tire, getting to work on time was not only in question, but getting there at all might be in jeopardy.

Okay, Andrea. What should I do next? She called her son back. "Hey, I won't be able to talk right now. Mommy has to fix her tire. I will have to call you later today." She hung up the phone. She was just about to figure out who to call next when a car pulled in behind hers.

"Hey, do you need help?"

Suddenly self-conscious that she was dressed for work in her scrubs with the big letters E-M-E-R-G-E-N-C-Y written across her back, Andrea wondered if most people would avoid her. "My gosh, yes! I didn't think anyone would stop because of my uniform. I have a flat. I can save someone's life in the Emergency Department, but I can't change a tire to save my own life."

"I can definitely change a tire," the man replied.

"Really, you can do that? I promise to maintain physical distancing."

The man chuckled. "Yeah. No problem. I am an off-duty tow truck driver."

The mystery man got to work, and Andrea asked, "Can I drive to work with this spare tire?"

"Where do you work?"

"I'm on my way to SickKids in Toronto."

"I wouldn't recommend it. That's a long way to drive on a spare. Do you have any other tires?"

"I have another set at home in my garage."

"Do you have CAA?" the man asked.

"Yes."

"Why not call them and have them meet you at your house and they can put on a proper tire?"

Andrea made the call. "We can have someone out there around quarter after nine," they assured.

"Oh . . . okay . . . thank you," Andrea stammered. She definitely wouldn't get to work on time. She called the hospital, apologizing profusely.

"Don't worry, Andrea. This is totally out of your control. Please don't stress."

As the kind gentleman finished putting on the spare, a tow truck passed them, slowing but then continuing on. "Are you good?" the stranger asked.

Am I good? she thought. It struck Andrea how good she actually was, considering. Usually when something like this happened, she would think it a catastrophic, end-of-the-world event. She would question, *How could this happen to me?* But instead, she felt uplifted. Despite this terrible inconvenience, she was still having a really good day. *This is humanity at its best*, she recognized.

Recently, Andrea had been discouraged. She had witnessed people being critical of grocery store staff, noticed others not following physical distancing rules, and viewed unkind messages online. However, seeing someone on a Saturday morning so willing to pull over and help her even though she was in uniform and considered a "plague nurse" by some . . . it was affirming and made her believe in the goodness of humankind again. Kindness really does supersede everything else. It reminded her of why she chose to be a nurse in the first place.

A text came in from CAA: **Tow truck will arrive at 8:36 a.m.** This was great news, much earlier than first expected.

"What's your name?" she asked the man just before he drove away. He answered, but with so much going on in her head, she was unable to process what he said or file his name permanently in her memory.

When Andrea got back to her house, the tow truck was already there.

"Hey, you're the person I saw at the side of the road. I almost stopped, but then I got this call."

"Yep, it's me."

He changed the spare, putting on a more permanent tire.

"I'll move out of the way so you can take off for work. I can clean up after you go," the tow truck drive offered. "Thank you for everything you do on the front line."

Andrea thanked him and took off for work.

We are all warriors, she thought. *Every single one of us. Whether we are out working to keep others fed or healthy or if we are social distancing at home. Even we first responders need help, too, sometimes. And we are so very grateful for it.*

Andrea parked and rushed in to start her shift. About to begin, she looked at her watch: 10:02 a.m. Could the day get any better? After all that, she was only two minutes late!

Andrea Logan is a nurse practitioner who lives in Innisfil, Ontario, with her son, Colby.

THANK-YOU LETTERS ARE NOT CANCELLED

By Catherine Kenwell

To my kind neighbours and first responders:

Oh gosh, where do I start? Thank you, first of all, to the "young gentleman" who picked up my eighty-eight-year-old stubborn-as-a-mule dad when he tripped and fell at the Blake Street Plaza today.

We appreciate your kindness and willingness to see him to his apartment building. I understand you said something to the effect of, "Forget COVID, I can't leave you here, can I help?" and you gently helped him to his feet. At a time when we're all so scared to be near other people lest we infect or be infected, you are the best kind of human—the best kind of brave, too.

Thank you to the woman who called 911; he was, of course, likely annoyed with you because he said he was fine (did I start this out by saying he's stubborn?). We appreciate your presence of mind in telling him he needed to be checked out.

To the young female paramedic, who bandaged him up and asked him the right questions (I'm a brain-injury survivor so I'm ready to jump on insufficient delivery of concussion protocol). I asked him to repeat the questions you asked, so thank you for your expertise and care. And for all of the work you've been doing, before and especially now.

To my dad's nosy neighbours, you know I thank you every day for looking out for my incredibly independent best friend. Thank you for asking about him. We love you.

You might say, after reading this far, "Why was your eighty-eight-year-old dad out in the first place? Doesn't he know how dangerous it is? Don't you do his shopping and look after him?"

Answer is, yes, we do. We take him meals and check his fridge and run his errands. He lives on his own, and we all live close by. He's not a child. He's smart. He's independent. He's in excellent shape for his age. And therein lies the crux of this. He is stubborn—he says he keeps his distance from others and disinfects and washes adequately. That's . . . good, I guess. We do everything he needs except for the two thing he craves and misses the most: fresh air and independence.

It's difficult, navigating this pandemic. Even more so for an eighty-eight-year-old. We're all doing our best.

And my dad will be fine, I think. He has a bump and a bandage on his head and some other minor cuts and bruises. He's at home, resting. And I checked his fridge and cupboards to see what else he doesn't need.

So in closing, thank you . . . young man, telephone woman, paramedic, neighbours . . . we feel extremely blessed to be in the company of such kind, good people. Even when it's supposed to be at a distance. If any of you happen to read this, will you please drop me a DM? I'd like to thank you more personally. You know, from a distance.

TRUCK STOPS ARE NOT CANCELLED

BY SONYA ANDERSON WITH JENNI WUTTUNEE

COVID-19 HAS EVERYONE REIMAGINING THEIR heroes. Front-line workers such as nurses, doctors, personal support workers, and grocery store employees are being hailed of late, but behind all these people is a different kind of hero that usually garners very little attention, even though they help keep the blood pumping through the entire system.

If you're grateful that your grocery shelves are stocked, and personal protective equipment is being delivered, then you have a truck driver to thank for keeping things rolling as much of the rest of the economy grinds to a halt.

While COVID-19 will be remembered as the pandemic that introduced us all to the world of social distancing, it has presented some challenges that uniquely affect truckers, from an inability to access drive-throughs to get much-needed coffee and meals, to finding restrooms that are open. The life of a trucker can feel isolating at the best of times, spending long days and often weeks away from their families, but during these troubling times truckers appear to have been left behind, struggling with limited resources to take care of even their most basic needs while on the road.

Reading about their challenges caused one hotel chain in the Prairies to step up and put a call out to commercial truckers through their Facebook page, offering them a complimentary hot shower and breakfast, dinner, or a muffin and coffee "to go" at their hotels in Saskatchewan and Manitoba.

The Holiday Inn Express in North Battleford, Saskatchewan, which opened its doors in 2019, decided, along with its sister hotels, the Western Star chain, to give back to an industry that's contributing so much to the Canadian economy.

"Even in the best of times people don't recognize the vital role that truckers play in our daily lives. And with them being in and out of so many businesses with their deliveries, it's really important that they have an opportunity to wash themselves off. The shower has been a big deal to the truckers that have come through," said director of sales and marketing Jenni Wuttunee.

"Breakfast is served, free of charge, from 5 to 10 a.m. and dinner is from 6 to 8 p.m., with hot coffee and a muffin served between those hours." Her hotel in North Battleford has set aside the showers and bathrooms on the first floor for arriving truckers. After each use, the showers and bathrooms are cleaned and disinfected in preparation for their next use.

Takeout meals are specially prepared by a dedicated staff member who uses utmost care to ensure they can maintain social distancing and hygiene while offering comfort food to the truckers that stop in.

Although truckers aren't normally part of their guest pool, usually sleeping in the bunks in their truck cabs, Wuttunee noted that they do supply all their inventory and hence are a critical part of their business's success.

Wuttunee marvels at how much her staff have benefitted from the gift of kindness their hotels have extended to truckers. It's often said that by giving, you get back far more than you could have ever imagined, and in a time when their hotel employees have been struggling with downsizing and worries about their own futures, the positivity and gratitude they've received from the truckers is a comforting salve that helps them know they are part of something wonderful in these crazy times.

Jenni Wuttunee is the director of sales and marketing for Holiday Inn Express & Suites in North Battleford, Saskatchewan.

RA33IT & BEAR ARE NOT CANCELLED

By Tara Shannon

"I'm afraid," said Rabbit.
"What are you afraid of?"
asked Bear.
"I don't know," replied Rabbit.
"I just am."

"Then, I will sit with
you until you're not
afraid anymore,"
said Bear.
"We will face it
together."

"I'M AFRAID," SAID RABBIT.

"What are you afraid of?" asked Bear.

"I don't know," replied Rabbit. "I just am."

"Then I will sit with you until you're not afraid anymore," said Bear. "We will face it together."

The post that went viral.

I BEGAN WRITING THIS THE day after tragedy struck Nova Scotia. A lone gunman opened fire, killing many and wounding several more—wounding the collective consciousness of the entire nation. A knife in our backs when we were already down, struggling to cope in this new world of COVID-19.

It's unreal.

I was mindlessly scrolling through Facebook when a notification caught my eye: **Tara Shannon we need Rabbit today**, it read. It was posted by someone I know through a writing group I've frequented now for the last two years. Without warning, tears began to flow down my cheeks, and for a minute I wondered what my little Rabbit could possibly offer amidst this tragedy.

I created Rabbit a year ago to bring hope and comfort to myself while I processed my own grief, loss, anxiety, and despair. From 2009 to 2013, I experienced a miscarriage, the end of my marriage, the loss of both my parents, and my own cancer diagnosis. To top it all off, while on medical EI, my job was terminated. It was a lot in a relatively short period of time, although I don't remember thinking of it like that then. I was more concerned with putting one foot in front of the other and moving forward no matter how graceful or ungraceful I was at doing so. In the back of my mind, I knew that sooner or later I would have to sort through all my feelings. Rabbit helped me do that, and I shared my simple drawings, paired up with equally simple dialogue, among my friends and family online. I had no expectations beyond that, only the hope that my words might be useful to someone else, somewhere along the line. A few short months later, and quite literally overnight, the whole world seemed to need my Rabbit.

I had almost given up on Rabbit back in the fall of 2019. I had attempted a Kickstarter campaign but didn't reach my goal. It seemed like Rabbit wasn't of interest to too many people, especially publishers. So I decided to regroup and try again, adapting the idea of Rabbit to a new character and story. The novel that resulted from that regrouping exercise currently sits with a publisher, and I (not so) patiently await their thoughts. In the meantime, and as I worked on my novel, Christmas came and went and COVID-19 loomed closer and closer. My anxiety started to grow, and I noticed that others seemed to be getting nervous, too. It was then that I realized some of my old Rabbit drawings might be worth sharing again. So I shared them once more to my social media, and if for no other reason than to bring myself calm, I started drawing some new ones, too. My usual friends and family commented and liked them, and life carried on.

One night as I readied for bed, I decided to scroll through Facebook one more time before turning my phone off and going to sleep. That's when I noticed a familiar sight: my Rabbit & Bear. But they hadn't been shared by me, they had been shared by a page I followed, which in turn had shared my image from a page I did not follow. I clicked through and was surprised to see that the image had several comments and likes and had been shared almost 7,000 times. Noticing I hadn't been tagged as the source, I commented, stating who I was and thanking the page admins for sharing my image. I then thanked all those who had commented and went to sleep.

The next morning, my image had been shared via that one page over 15,000 times. The number of shares continued to grow, and then my friends began messaging me letting me know they had seen my drawing on other pages and shared by their friends and family. I was amazed. My little Rabbit, speaking with its Bear friend, had gone viral.

The admin from Heart of the Warrior Woman messaged to tell me that my post had brought the page the most shares in its history, and another admin messaged to let me know that over 1.5 million saw my post on the Mindfulness Ireland page.

I was stunned. My Rabbit?

Messages started pouring in from people across Canada and from all around the world including India, Australia, Ireland, the United States, Israel, Africa, Honduras, Germany, Portugal, Spain, Italy, and China. All of them wanting to let me know just how much Rabbit & Bear meant to them and asking how they could find more. I began sharing daily, both new and old messages from Rabbit, and all the while heartfelt messages and requests continued to flow through my inbox and in the comments. A newspaper reporter in Honduras interviewed me for a future article . . . the American Childhood Cancer Organization requested a drawing tutorial . . . a widow in Ohio asked if

Rabbit could say something about how it felt to be so alone and to miss the ones they loved . . . a lady from Rainbow, Australia, asked if Rabbit could say something about storms and how, when they're over, a rainbow always appears . . . and several counsellors and psychologists have reached out asking if they could use Rabbit when working with their clients, especially children. Rabbit was bringing hope and comfort to so many struggling with fear, grief, depression, and anxiety—all of the things I had struggled with over the years. All of the things that led to the creation of my Rabbit a year ago.

It was bittersweet. A year ago, Rabbit's voice was small, fighting to be heard. Now, as COVID-19 spreads throughout our world, so many people understand Rabbit in a way they hadn't before. The timing wasn't right a year ago for Rabbit to meet the world. The fact that it's the right time now fills me with equal amounts of sadness and joy. I'm sad because of what we are facing as a nation and a worldwide community. I feel joy because my work, simple as it may be, is bringing comfort to so many. As a writer that is what we truly want . . . to be relevant and to make a difference to someone, even if it's only just one someone.

The fact that Rabbit, along with Bear, has reached so many is humbling. At this time of great uncertainty, I am being given a gift. I don't know what's in the cards next for Rabbit & Bear or the novel I have written or anything else in my life, for that matter. But I am excited to see what might happen next. I have hope, and that's something I've been working on and wishing for, for a long time.

"Make a wish," said the dandelions.

"But where will you go?" asked Rabbit.

"We will become your wish and one day we will return to you," replied the dandelions.

"You mean you won't die?" Rabbit asked.

"No," laughed the dandelions. "A wish can never die. It can only come true."

The first Rabbit I ever created.

NEVER LOSE HOPE AND NEVER stop wishing. You just never know when that wish might come true.

© 2020 Tara Shannon. Used with permission.

Tara Shannon lives in southern Ontario with her family and many beloved pets. She's a freelance writer, aspiring author, and creator of the illustrated characters Rabbit & Bear. As a cancer survivor and mental health advocate, Tara hopes to help others see that wishes do come true and that magic really does exist. Find her on Facebook and Instagram @tarashannonwrites and @bearessentially on Twitter.

INGENUITY IS NOT CANCELLED

By Catherine Kenwell with Dr. Sarah Waterston

DR. SARAH WATERSTON KNOWS FIRST-HAND how important hand sanitizer is within the health care sector. As a pediatrician with Quinte Health Care and Belleville General Hospital, she sees its impact every workday, especially during COVID-19.

So it made sense that early on, Sarah was concerned about supplies and shortages of such an important tool in the fight against the coronavirus. But unlike many doctors on the front lines, she was in a unique position to offer a solution.

In addition to her medical practice, Sarah is also a co-owner of Kinsip House of Fine Spirits, a family-operated small-batch distillery in Bloomfield, Prince Edward County.

When Sarah noticed a shrinking supply of hand sanitizer at work, she jumped into action by offering up Kinsip's production facilities. Her farm-based, grain-to-glass distillery's production lines usually include small-batch gins, vodkas, whiskys, and rums. Now, Kinsip is producing high-proof alcohol-based hand sanitizers to fight against the pandemic, and has worked with Health Canada and with federal excise tax to be able to make the shift in production.

Distilleries are well positioned to be hand sanitizer producers because the key ingredient in their products is food-grade grain alcohol (yes, the stuff you can drink in your cocktails). Adding hydrogen peroxide and glycerine creates an excellent sanitizer. Kinsip was one of the first Ontario distilleries to make the switch in production, and they have been providing their new product to local health care workers and the public.

"It's a difficult time for everyone," says Sarah. "In health care, we're preparing for the effects of COVID-19 and working to still support and treat our patients for other issues, while avoiding in-person visits whenever possible. Social distancing and hand-washing are most important, but in hospitals and long-term care homes, sanitizer is important for health care workers and patients alike. As a doctor, I'm continually doing hand hygiene. I often need to perform hand hygiene at moments when a sink is not accessible—hand sanitizer is essential for those moments."

Conversely, social distancing is difficult for small businesses, and Sarah notes that Prince Edward County, renowned and loved as a tourist destination, will be especially devastated. "It's worrisome. Distilleries in Ontario are highly taxed; we pay ten times the tax that small Ontario wineries, breweries, and cideries do. Craft distilling in Ontario is unsustainable even in booming tourism years. But without tourism in the region, it becomes a critical situation. All local businesses, directly tourism-related or not, are going to be extremely hard hit."

Now, in addition to providing sanitizers to local front-line health care workers, Kinsip includes a small bottle with each online order of spirits.

"It's a community effort," Sarah explains. "Our shop is open for pickup only; we're encouraging people to order online and have their products shipped to their home across Ontario or take advantage of curbside pickup. We are including a bottle of hand sanitizer with online purchases as a small thank you for supporting Kinsip and social distancing and to give people a tool to help perform hand hygiene even when a sink isn't accessible. As small business owners, we're struggling like everyone else, but as a doctor, I will tell you, social distancing is key if we're going to win this battle and move forward with our 'new normal.'

"Throughout all of the work—preparing and completely changing how we practice medicine, how Kinsip functions, and how I'm living socially distanced—I've found myself so aware of the supportive teams and community that I am part of. Although we are physically distanced, I feel closer and more connected to the various teams and communities that I am a part of," Sarah reflects. "We really are all in this together."

Dr. Sarah Waterston is a pediatrician with Quinte Health Care and Belleville General Hospital.

SIMPLICITY IS NOT CANCELLED

By Mandy Johnson

NEVER BEFORE HAVE WE BEEN reduced to the most basic of our modern existence: no work, no social interaction, no travel, no shopping . . . no distractions. Let's be honest, the old saying "be careful what you wish for" has actually come true. Our busyness has contributed to more of everything: more stuff, more stress, more obligation, more expectation. That frantic state that keeps us distracted is the foundation for a wish for simplicity and some time off. What we didn't bargain for is the pandemic that put the planet on shutdown, or rather a government-imposed foreclosure on everything we know as normal. There is not a person on this earth who hasn't hoped for a break in the race that we willingly run day in, day out. The COVID-19 pandemic has granted us all the "gift" of time, and for most of us, the struggle has been bitter and uneasy.

For years I have personally struggled with the ideal of simplifying. From my vantage point, the need to Marie Kondo your life is really about an honest relationship with your stuff. Not only are we the physical gatherers of material goods, but we are also the mental collectors of bad decisions, bad relationships, and bad choices about our health and general well-being. It becomes more evident in our silence and inactivity that we have "looked for love in all the wrong places." We spend most of life wishing for peace, personally and globally, but we fill every empty beat with stuff. I can't help but think that simplicity is the opposite of the worldly Pandora's box that masks itself as a gift but is truly a curse. We are operating mindlessly, creating complicated lives that seem beyond our control. But, like many events and choices, we are very much making decisions that layer our existence with the stress of more. Taking responsibility and owning our choices is a difficult and sobering process. Finding those things that truly feed our souls requires a connection beyond the ordinary. The Instagram world of today presents a filtered existence that is more entertainment than enlightenment, and we often get caught in distinguishing between the two. I need to check myself often to stay present and conscious and remind myself of the paradox of the simple. As with all our choices, there is an opportunity cost we all pay for decisions we make. I personally have found the consequences of willingly complicating my life heavy and stressful, and as a result, I personally have struggled with finding happiness in all the wrong places.

When the threat of the COVID-19 pandemic became a reality and the response to this virus became a global shutdown, I couldn't help but feel that this unprecedented pause would strip us down to the bottom of Maslow's hierarchy and remind us of the need to adjust and consciously move toward a more meaningful life. We have all had to simplify our lives to the basic—satisfying physiological and safety needs first. For most of us, that is a place we have taken for granted. Our excess has removed the concept of scarcity and simple existence. It's no coincidence that the events in our lives are cumulative, teachable moments. This pandemic was a major shout-out from the planet that our lives as we knew them had to change, amid imposed restrictions that would be rife with a global grief for more than just our physical freedom. For me, COVID-19 provided the exclamation point to my search for simplicity.

Life's events often speak to your conscious iterations of what needs to shift. The topic of simplifying has been an internal dialogue for a while now, but a recent unfortunate family tragedy had knocked the wind out of me and forced the conversation of simplicity to the forefront of my thoughts. The previous summer, I got the crushing news that my younger sister, Kim, had passed away. I had raced from my home to join my mother, and together we had the painful task of saying goodbye to Kim for the last time. The business of celebrating a life cut too short was difficult and heartbreaking. Death has a way of stripping all the inessential away, and the rawness and finality offer some clarity, albeit through tear-stained cheeks. In life, we falsely measure our legacy in accomplishments and tangible items. However, in death, there is no value in those things. Comfort lies in a life well lived . . . a life that was full of experiences, memories, family, and love. It was, at that time, that my thoughts travelled to the meaning of life, of her life. My mom and I spent months going through a lifetime of paperwork and pictures, a house full of stuff. It was overwhelming every time we entered the home and made decisions about what to keep, what to sell, what to do with all the "stuff." There were boxes and boxes, unopened from previous moves physically filling rooms and closets. Of course, there were some sentimental keepsakes that we held closely and kept in memory. But the mountains of items that we parted with held no energy, no DNA, no emotional value. I couldn't help but think that I, too, had to work through the emotional and physical collections I have carried for decades.

Intellectually, we understand that our health and happiness don't reside in the clothes, pictures, furniture, and items we stuff into our finite spaces, but we continue to collect more and more as if to insulate our souls and create abundance. There is some temporary comfort in excess of any kind. There is a soulful grief, though, in the reconciliation that those choices just complicate our innate desire to find connection with our innermost search for contentment. We are so uncomfortable with the word *simple*. We have given it a bad rap. We have labelled the pursuit of a simple life as undesirable, maybe even pedestrian. We meditate, we budget, we declutter in search of elusive mental and physical peace only to race to the shops, engage in complicated relationships, and torture ourselves with what our lives *should* look like.

My sister's passing was not my original motivation to simplify, but it certainly was part of my hyperfocus to move forward in my goal to zero-base what has become a heavy life. The isolation and mandatory lockdown of COVID-19 certainly assisted in what was going to be part of a new relationship with my being. I am not suggesting that this time was not without fear of what was changing both externally and internally. Collectively we could tangibly feel the fear for a world that once was and for what would take its place. As the weeks pressed on and the reality and severity progressed, the tension of change was felt in every conversation, both spoken and unspoken. Every unnecessary expense was reduced or eliminated, household income evaporated, physical exercise and movement were reformatted to home workouts, meals were cooked, friends were called, and we sat in silence or in a Netflix daze that became dull and void of entertainment. We all have had more time to think, to challenge, to fear, to sleep, to talk to God as if we have had a death sentence placed on our lives. The wish for "time" gave us our opportunity to truly and honestly inventory the decisions that have left us vulnerable and those that have left us insulated.

I believe the desire for a simple life resides in all of us, and that does not mean a life void of challenges and opportunities. What a global pandemic has taught us all is that much healing can happen in this pause. The planet and all of its residents have experienced a global wake-up call. Making life easy is the most difficult thing. But if we check our motivations, our goals, our wish for personal and universal health and happiness . . . the answer lies in the uncomplicated, quiet, elementary activities and pursuits. For many, the promise to re-enter this world after the pandemic will require a simple approach to what we need to be healthy, happy, and fulfilled. Simplicity is not going without. Simplicity is honouring what is within. It's a discipline that honours our most basic needs. Simplicity offers healthy appraisal of a life travelled with unnecessary baggage, and I will consciously go forward on my next adventure with a carry-on.

Mandy Johnson is a mother of two great children, Shae and Tie. She has called Barrie, Ontario, home for the past thirty-five years. Mandy is part of a family real estate business with her husband, Ross. She spends her free time doing yoga, modelling, freelance writing, and working with community charities and groups whenever possible. You can find her on Instagram @mjohnson_harris or on Facebook by searching Mandy Johnson.

PAYING IT FORWARD IS NOT CANCELLED

By Heather Down with Patti Hilton

TERRA WAS WORKING AT THE salad bar in the Antigonish Superstore, a grocery-and-more retailer, when she got the surprise of her life. Antigonish is a small Nova Scotia town, consisting mostly of well-known locals and students from the local university, St. Francis Xavier, or St. FX for short. She did not recognize the man who handed her ten envelopes, but she wouldn't soon forget his generosity.

"Can I help you, sir?" she had asked.

"I just want to say thank you to the staff for working in these strange times," he said as he handed over the envelopes, each bearing a handwritten message of gratitude.

A little taken aback, Terra asked, "Can I get your name?"

"I would like to remain anonymous. But these are for the workers here." And with that, he turned and scurried out the door.

Terra took the envelopes to the store manager, Patti.

"What's this?" Patti asked.

"A man came in and gave me these. I didn't know who he was. I know a lot of people around here, but I couldn't place him. He said to give these to the staff, and he said thank you for working during the coronavirus to keep us fed."

"Thank you, Terra," Patti replied and laid the envelopes on her desk, each one decorated with a personal message: Thank you . . . We are grateful . . . Thank you for everything . . .

Patti tore open an envelope and $40 cash fell out. *Wow,* she thought. *We simply come in to do our job, what we normally do every day.* For someone to recognize the value of what she and her colleagues were doing was pretty overwhelming. It was a feel-good moment she couldn't ignore. She opened the next envelope, and again, $40 was inside. There was $400 cash in total. Patti took in a deep breath and blinked back the tears. It was obvious there still was good to be found in humanity.

The next day at the morning huddle—a staff meeting where she and her colleagues communicated about what would be going on that day, imparted information about sales, and talked about anything new—Patti shared the story of the envelopes.

"A man came in yesterday and gave these ten envelopes to Terra. He wouldn't leave his name and he wanted to remain a mystery. Each envelope had a lovely gratitude message on it and $40 inside. I am looking for input on how we should distribute this very kind gift of appreciation," she said as she looked out over the staff members. It was obvious they were astonished by this beautiful gesture.

Corey piped up. "Why don't we pay it forward? Maybe donate it to some seniors who could really use it for food?"

"Great idea," Rob affirmed.

"Yes, let's do that," another colleague added. And soon the room was abuzz, people chiming in on how this would be the best use of the funds.

It was unanimous. The staff at Antigonish's Superstore were going to donate increments of $100 to four seniors. Although fairly new as the manager at this particular location, Patti knew she had made the right choice to come here. She couldn't help herself: she was proud of the decision this group of colleagues had made to take a good situation and make it better. It was comforting to know that even though these were scary times, paying it forward wasn't cancelled.

Patti's next step was to get in contact with a community liaison who could choose four deserving seniors, take their orders, and coordinate fulfillment. She had no trouble finding the perfect person for the job, and project pay-it-forward was put into motion.

The truth is, we all depend on food. And those producing, transporting, and selling life-saving sustenance are, in fact, true superheroes in every single way.

Patti Hilton is the manager at the Superstore in Antigonish, Nova Scotia.

APPRECIATION IS NOT CANCELLED

BY CATHERINE KENWELL

LAST MONDAY MORNING, WE PATIENTLY waited for our waste collectors. We listened for the trucks, and when they turned the corner onto our street, we headed out to greet them. We'd carefully clipped a little baggie onto one of our garbage bags.

In the baggie was a bright purple and blue homemade thank-you card. Inside, we wrote a note saying, "Thank you. Coffee's on us today!" and we included a Tim Horton's gift card worth $5, covering the price of an extra-large coffee for each of them.

While we stood inside our front porch, we watched as one worker peered curiously at the bag, unclipped it, read it, and looked in our window. We waved, and he gave us a big smile and a thumbs-up. He then showed his partner and his partner gave us a wave and a smile.

It felt pretty darn good to make genuine eye contact and share smiles with these guys, and to be able to show our appreciation "in person." During our self-isolation, they are still out working, picking up smelly, rotten goodness-knows-what, and even more of it now since we're all at home. Adding to that, although the guys are wearing PPEs, they are exposed to anything virus-y that might be lurking in our trash.

Tim Horton's has an online gift card app, from which you can personalize and print any denomination. It's a little bit, and we're not saving the world, but if we can buy a coffee and put a smile on an essential worker's face, why the heck not?

MUSIC IS NOT CANCELLED

BY HEATHER DOWN WITH JASON MCCOY AND JIM PAYETTA

JIM PAYETTA, A MUSICIAN, SONGWRITER, marketer, and co-owner of the Barrie Colts, an Ontario Hockey League team, found himself at home, facing a different pace of life because of the public health directives.

When Jim was enjoying his morning coffee during his second week of isolation, he decided to poke around online. *Look at all these various artists, from Keith Urban to John Legend, doing concerts from their homes for their fans*, he mused.

It struck Jim that this was a great concept—artists doing their best to entertain and stay connected with people. It was about music, their craft of creating it, and maintaining a connection with those who wanted to hear it.

And if ever there was a world event that demonstrated the simple truth that we are all connected . . . this pandemic surely was it!

He began to ponder some more. It really was amazing that a virus that spread across the globe started with just one person. Talk about the Power of One!

Jim was struck with an idea. He picked up the phone and called his friend and occasional songwriting partner, notable Canadian country singer Jason McCoy.

Jason is a very talented songwriter, singer, and artist—not to mention accomplished. His list of awards include two-time Male Vocalist of the Year at the Canadian Country Music Awards, three SOCAN Song of the Year Awards, nineteen CCMA nominations, five Juno nominations for Best Country Male Vocalist, a Global Artist Award at the CMA Awards in Nashville, and three-time CCMA Group of the Year with the Road Hammers—plus a Juno for best country recording.

Jim and Jason had recently successfully collaborated on a song called "Zamboni," which had been recorded by Jason's band, the Road Hammers.

"Hey, Jason," Jim began. "What if we could get one song, a song that was about hope, about the human spirit, about the Power of One, about the fact that we are all connected . . . what if we could get not only well-known artists and singers, but every person who wanted to participate, to record their own versions and share them? How fast could we make that one song spread all over the world? Using technology and the Power of One, it's possible."

Jason, well connected and motivated, was the conduit to make this project a reality. A mere four days later, they had their first demo of the song "We Are One," and within a week, Jason was reaching out to musicians he knew to join the project.

Initially Jason asked his band to contribute, but he also felt it was really important to include people not only from across Canada but from across the world as well, demonstrating the message of the song: we are all connected. Accomplished and well-known musicians from Greece to India to Sweden to Austria all participated. Here at home, the roster included many Canadian musicians such as vocalist Aaron Pritchett, guitarist Darren Savard, and Barenaked Ladies front man Ed Robertson, just to name a few.

But Jason felt this song needed a choir. He really wanted the Harlem Gospel Choir; New York, after all, was currently the epicentre of the pandemic. Jason had no idea how to make that happen. His daughter, however, did. She managed to find some contact information online and Jason reached out. He was both shocked and pleased when Anna Bailey, the manager of the choir, got back to him, excited about the project. The choir recorded their parts in isolation and sent them in.

The song was written and produced, the website called WeAre1World.net was created, and a video was masterfully put together in a two-and-a-half-week whirlwind. And it is spectacular!

In the video, Jason encourages people to create and record their own rendition of the song and post it online using the hashtag #weare1worldsong.

Anyone can go to the site and download the tracks for free. There are choices of tracks as well, depending on whether or not you want just the backing tracks, or even if you want all the stem tracks separately.

Besides spreading hope and affording an opportunity for fun and creativity during lockdown, this song is also a fundraiser for COVID-19 relief initiatives. The more the song is recorded and played, the more royalties are produced and donated to the cause. There are also donate buttons on the website for anyone who wants to contribute directly.

One small idea, one single phone call, one fleeting thought acted upon can make such a huge difference worldwide, proving that, in fact, "We Are One."

Jason McCoy is a country singer who is extremely proud to be involved with this project and is excited to see something created in his hometown of Barrie go around the world to make such an impact. He always knew music had the power to touch people's lives, but it was another thing to see it on a global scale. For more information or if you wish to download "We Are One," please visit WeAre1World.net

Jim Payetta is an entrepreneur who began his career as a musician and songwriter. Jim left the music business to start an advertising agency, which led him into many other avenues, including the media business, private wealth management, and even a car racing track. He is currently a part-owner of the OHL Barrie Colts hockey team.

We are 1 world.NET
One world. One Song. Your Voice.

WE ARE ONE
Written by Jason McCoy and Jim Payetta

INTRO –C/G

VERSE 1

C   AM
A WORLD OF WORRY, A WORLD OF CHANGE, A WORLD OF LIVES, RE-ARRANGED

       F   C
JOINED TOGETHER IN SONG, WE ARE ONE (we are one) WE ARE ONE (we are one)

C   AM
WE HAVE DOUBTS, WE HAVE FEARS, WE SHARE THE HURT, WE SHARE THE TEARS

       F   C
WE ARE HERE, WE'RE NOT ALONE, WE ARE ONE (we are one) WE ARE ONE (we are one)

CHORUS

AM   F   AM   G
MILES MAY DIVIDE US, BUT LOVE (MUSIC 2nd time) WILL UNITE US

      AM   F   C
WE WILL RISE, AND OVERCOME, WE ARE ONE (we are one) WE ARE ONE (we are one)

AM   F   C   G
ONE WORLD, ONE FIGHT, ONE HEART, ONE LIFE, UNDER ONE SUN

AM   F   C
ONE BREATH, ONE SKY, ONE SONG, ONE CRY RAISE YOUR VOICE AND SING

G   AM   F   C
ALONG… WE ARE ONE (we are one) WE ARE ONE (we are one) WE ARE ONE (we are one)

WE ARE ONE (we are one)

VERSE 2

C   AM
KEEP THE FAITH, TAKE A STAND, AND BE STILL ACROSS THE LAND

       F   C
WE WILL WIN, THIS WILL BE DONE, WE ARE ONE (we are one) WE ARE ONE (we are one)

C   AM
DO YOUR PART, EASE THE PAIN, STAY APART, BREAK THE CHAIN,

       F   C
WE'LL JOIN HANDS, WHEN FREEDOM COMES, WE ARE ONE (we are one) WE ARE ONE (we are one)

2nd CHORUS

OUT (REPEAT)

   AM   F   C
OOOOOO …. OOOOO…OOOOO WE ARE ONE (we are one) WE ARE ONE (we are one)

CUPCAKES AND CRAFTS ARE NOT CANCELLED

BY ERIN PATERSON

IT WAS HARD TO IMAGINE a pandemic was going on as my daughter and I explored the wooded ravine. We walked along dirt pathways as Canada geese flew overhead and robins greeted us from the trees. We traipsed through the bushes, burrs sticking to our pants, to peer at the rushing stream below. Anxious to see what lay ahead, my daughter ran to the crest of a hill. I could see the pompoms on the top of her turquoise winter hat bouncing up and down in the distance. By the time I'd caught up with her, she had gathered up pine cones, fuzzy cattails, and stones, which she held out in her pink mittened hands for a picture. I could see the thrill of discovery in her eyes. This wonderful place was so close to our home, yet I had never taken her here before. We were enjoying the first spring-like weather, the warm sun hitting our backs. The snow had melted only a few days before. By the time we headed home for hot chocolate, our shoes were covered in mud. For one blissful hour, the fact that the entire world was on edge as a new virus circled the globe wasn't on our minds.

In the past week alone, our schools were closed down, extracurricular activities were cancelled, and people were told to work from home. Retail stores and restaurants started closing and laying off their employees. Air traffic was restricted, and Canada's borders were shut. Each day there was a new announcement on television from the prime minister, who was in self-isolation because his wife was sick with COVID-19. We were told to practise social distancing, and suddenly going to the grocery store became laden with risk. We were all fearful of catching a virus that could overwhelm our health care system and cause many deaths. There was, and continues to be, so much uncertainty about our future.

My family, like everyone else's, has been trying to adjust to the sudden changes. My brother and his family from BC cancelled their visit because they were nervous that they might get stuck in Ontario with us. When my mom injured her knee and was unable to walk, we had second thoughts about taking her to the hospital. She is living with us as she recovers; at least we know she is safe. My father and my mother-in-law both live in retirement homes that have gone into lockdown. My husband, who works in construction, is still on the job, and I am nervous for his safety. I am trying to entertain my daughter while working from home.

Despite everything that is going on, it is not all bad. Gone is the early morning rush. No more packing lunches and prodding my daughter out the door so we can get to school before the morning bell rings. My commute to work is now just a walk down the hall to my home office. Gone is the stress of getting dinner on the table and homework done so I can get my daughter to bed on time. We have a break from the drama of the schoolyard and bullies. There is no pressure to go anywhere or to visit anyone because we are not supposed to. Instead, we have long days stretched out before us.

Knowing we would have to get creative to fill those days, I enlisted my daughter for help. I rolled out a long piece of paper on the living room floor and grabbed some coloured markers. Then we sat together for a half hour, coming up with a gigantic list of fun things to do. The six-foot-long scroll is now hanging from the wall. Each day we pick an item off the list and put a bright yellow check mark next to it when it's done.

One day we flipped through a cookbook that had sat unused on the bookshelf for years and picked out an elaborate banana cupcake recipe. My daughter and I spent an hour in the kitchen roasting bananas in the oven, measuring the dry ingredients in a silver mixing bowl and the wet ingredients in another. Then we whipped up some egg whites and folded them into the mixture, scooping it all into muffin tins and watching them bake. We served them for dessert that night.

We spent three afternoons working on a papier mâché volcano in the basement. We created the structure out of a recycled pop bottle, an empty cracker box, and painter's tape. Then we cut up strips of old newspaper and dipped them in a goopy mix of flour and water. We both had fun sticking our hands into the slimy substance, pulling out dripping pieces of paper, and rubbing them flat. After it dried, we painted our volcano brown and green, with golden lava dripping down the sides. It was satisfying to make something together. Next we plan on creating our own volcanic eruption with baking soda and vinegar.

Each day after I have finished work, we make sure to go outside. I walk and my daughter rides her scooter next to me. First, we head over to the construction site at the end of our street where they are installing gigantic new sewer pipes. We wave to the four guys working behind the chain-link fence, and we peer into the deep hole in the middle of the road. Our trips are to see what is going on as much as it's an excuse for my daughter to ride her scooter on the plywood ramp running over the broken section of sidewalk. We wander the streets of our neighbourhood for an hour each day. More people are out just like us, pushing their babies in strollers or walking their dogs. They wave and move to the other side of the street so we can pass each other safely because of social distancing. Half the people we see are wearing masks on their faces. In a community where people rarely left their houses or cars, where the neighbours barely know each other, people are now strolling around and saying hello to one another.

It almost feels as if we have stepped back in time and we are living the slower paced, less chaotic life of my childhood. Where the neighbours were friendly and shops were closed on Sundays. When our days weren't packed with obligations and kids had free time. When there was less traffic on the roads and fewer planes in the sky. Where technology and social media didn't interfere with our lives. When we lived fully instead of viewing everything through a screen.

COVID-19 has brought a lot of negatives into our lives, and I have no doubt that things are going to get worse before they get better. For now, I am grateful for the opportunity to slow down and have more time to connect with my daughter. I am finally the type of parent I have always wanted to be, which our fast-paced society seemed to make impossible. Perhaps when this crisis is over, we will all emerge with a better understanding of who is truly important to us and what we really want out of our lives.

Toronto author Erin Paterson tested gene positive for Huntington's disease in 2006. Despite the diagnosis she was determined to have a family and live a joyful life. Erin has written for the Huntington Society of Canada (HSC) and spoke at the HSC youth conference for the past two years. A columnist for HuntingtonsDiseaseNews. com, she has also been published on TheMighty.com, Adopt4Life. com, and CanadaAdopts.com. She is currently looking for a publisher for her memoir titled All Good Things. *You can find out more at ErinPaterson.com.*

FAITH IS NOT CANCELLED

BY HEATHER DOWN WITH RENE AND TRACY SEGURA

HUSBAND AND WIFE TEAM RENE and Tracy ran a unique café. It was a coffee shop at the front, with Rene being the first point of contact, and it was a business centre at the back, complete with a full-colour copier, a place to network, and the offerings of Tracy's graphic design services. The couple did everything together—they worked together, they hung out together, and they even grocery shopped together. Sometimes their customers would ask how they did it, being together 24/7. Tracy would answer, "I don't know, but it works for us. We will be with each other on an eight-hour shift, then be like 'What do you want to do after work?'"

Although they stringently followed all the government directives, Tracy was a little skeptical of the news that played on a constant loop in the café. The coronavirus was just starting to spread beyond many borders. According to the news, it seemed those most affected were the elderly, and symptoms appeared to be flu-like.

I wonder if the news is trying to scare us? she briefly thought as she switched off the TV that had bombarded her with comments and images, that had attempted to ravage her peace of mind. Little did she know, her fleeting thought was very mistaken.

In a matter of days, the rules changed quickly, and the café was open only for takeout, so Tracy went to work while Rene stayed home. Rene went to pick up their girls from school, and the wind felt like it was ripping through him. He shuddered. *I feel a headache coming on*, he thought.

The forty-one-year-old couldn't sleep for days and had a mild headache—then he developed a tickle in his throat a week later along with shortness of breath. He was having difficulty breathing simply walking from the bed to the washroom, so they decided to seek medical attention. When they arrived at the assessment clinic, Rene was issued a mask. With being short of breath to begin with and trying to breathe through the mask, a panic attack ensued. Tracy soothed him but could not accompany him throughout the entire process. However, despite the attack, the medical staff was able to assess him, take his temperature, and, using the guidelines at the time (and with community spread not really being a thing yet), they sent him home. The couple had not travelled out of the country.

"It's probably a cold," they said.

When Rene emerged, Tracy asked, "Are we going to the hospital?"

"No. They think it is a cold. I have a cold, Trace." It was a strange mixture of confusion and relief. Tracy was not quite satisfied but also wanted desperately to believe the news was true.

Tracy dropped him home and went back to work at the café, but she kept checking on Rene at home. "How are you doing?" she would ask.

"I'm getting dressed."

"Oh, okay. Why? Are you going somewhere, or do you just want to get out of your pyjamas and freshen up?"

"I don't know," came the befuddled answer. "But I have to get dressed."

When Tracy got home, she looked at Rene and said, "I'm worried about you. You are acting confused."

Rene was irritated by this. "I have a cold, Trace. I haven't slept for days. Of course, I'm confused."

"I know you're upset, Rene. I'm going to shelve it for now, but tomorrow if you are still like this, we are going to have to go see a doctor or something."

As Tracy lay in bed beside her husband, she couldn't help but wonder if she should leave him to go to work tomorrow. A fleeting dark image flew through her brain that she might come home and find something sinister. She brushed it off.

They awoke at 1:30 a.m., and Rene was having great difficulty breathing. He didn't look good at all—he couldn't sleep, and he was extremely stressed.

After a couple of hours, Tracy said, "We have to take you to the hospital."

"No, Trace. It's just a cold."

Tracy grabbed him and said assertively, "We have to go. If we waste five hours sitting at the hospital to listen to a second doctor say you have a cold, I need to hear that. Please do this for me right now. I need to know that you have a cold."

He stopped arguing, and they set out for the hospital.

When they arrived, it was apparent how much the COVID-19 protocols and directives had escalated in a matter of a week. They were stopped between the two sliding glass doors leading into the Emergency Department. A set of three personnel triaged anyone who walked through.

"What are your symptoms?" they asked.

The couple told the medical staff what had been going on.

Then Tracy's sense of relief about getting help changed to anxiety when one of them said, "Rene, you need to come in. Tracy, you cannot come with him."

"What do you mean I can't come in?" she questioned.

He needs me, she thought. *What about his panic attacks? I have to help keep him calm.*

"We are really sorry. We know this is very hard. But you *cannot* come in."

Tracy burst into tears. Rene didn't want to go in. They went back outside and sat on a bench.

"I'm not going in alone," Rene said. "It's just a cold. Let's just go home."

A part of Tracy wanted to go home, too. They could go back to the safety of their house, lie down, and rest comfortably. She could take care of Rene. But she knew that would be selfish. She had to be strong for him. She grabbed his face. "Rene, you have to go in. You have to get checked out. Everything is going to be fine. Just go in. I won't leave this spot, and if things are too difficult, you can always come back outside, and I will be here."

They walked back into the hospital. "I can't go with you," Tracy said, more to convince herself than to inform Rene.

"He will be in really good hands. We will take very good care of him."

Although he was panicked, the nurses worked their miracles, helping Rene to remain calm and to relax. His oxygen levels were low, so he was given oxygen and tested for COVID-19.

About an hour after her husband entered the hospital, Tracy received a text from Rene, letting her know he was being admitted: **Go home, they are keeping me**. Reluctantly she went home.

After the first night spent in ER Trauma, Rene's condition did not seem to be improving. His diagnosis was severe bilateral pneumonia, a very bad case for his age. The glass doors on Rene's room allowed him to see into another room where a gentleman had just been brought in. The man coded and Rene watched as doctors, nurses, and other personnel scurried to the aid of this patient. Tragically, the man did not survive.

It was at this moment that Rene decided to activate his faith and prayed as if he were disputing death itself. "That is not going to be me. I am going home . . . I have a son, two daughters, and my wife to get to. I draw a line between me and death, it will not come near me."

Rene was surprised to see the ICU doctor, as he knew him from their business. He came down to see him. They chatted about coffee and Rene was able to relax before getting the news. "You know what? We are going to have to intubate you, but don't worry. That's my team right there, and we're going to take good care of you. You are in good hands. Right now, I want you to call your wife and let her know we are not sure how long it is going to take. It might take a week, it might take a day, you know. Might take longer, but you will not have any contact with her.

You won't be able to speak with her because you are going to be sedated."

Tracy had been informed by the hospital that her husband was going to be put on supportive care. She was told his body was very tired, which was true. He hadn't slept in over a week and a half, he hadn't eaten much—she knew he was down at least ten pounds going into the hospital. His body just didn't have the strength right now.

Rene FaceTimed Tracy: "I'm going to be away for a bit. Don't cry, Tracy. Tell Bri I am going to miss her birthday, but I'll see her after."

Monday was daughter Bri's tenth birthday. Rene had never missed a single birthday, and every year he always bought his girls roses. He was keenly aware that he wouldn't be home this time. It was a hard conversation to have.

Tracy called the kids down to say goodnight to their daddy. He was going to go to sleep for a little bit, and she reminded them they needed to be strong for him.

That Saturday night in the washroom, Tracy screamed and whispered at the same time, *You can't have him. You have to give him back to me.* A voice inside her said, *He's going to be okay.*

Sunday morning, a nurse called. Her name was Mary. "He's awake. We give him a bit of a sedation vacation once in a while. He won't remember it, but it gives us the chance to check his brain activity and communication. He told me the names of all the continents. He told me he was from El Salvador and I found out he liked Spanish music. So I put on some Spanish music for him."

Tracy was shocked that he was awake and so incredibly grateful and awed by this nurse's compassion. She had taken the time to find out all these things by asking questions. The amount of care she exhibited was incredible, and the news brightened Tracy's entire day.

Tracy made sure roses were delivered for Bri's birthday. Classmates made handmade cards and dropped them at the porch throughout the day. While sitting on the steps inside her house, Tracy noticed some balloons. *Probably from one of Bri's friends,* she thought.

Bri opened the door and screamed, "It's my cousins!"

Rene's brother and sister-in-law had driven an hour and a half with their four young kids to stand on the lawn with a banner that read: HAPPY BIRTHDAY, BRI. The emotion was electric. They wanted desperately to hug and cry, but they kept their distance.

That night Bri told her mom, "God is taking care of Dad. My birthday wish is that he will get better and he will."

The next morning, the improved Rene was taken off life support. As he became more aware of his surroundings, seeing the machines and tubes, anxiety started to creep up. He wasn't fully comprehending that he was getting better.

During a FaceTime exchange, Rene said: "Tracy I don't think it looks good for me."

"Look at my face. You know me. You are doing so much better than what you were. You don't recall what you went through in the last seventy-two hours, but I do. Look at me. I am telling you the truth. You are doing fantastic."

Tracy knew that Rene's mental health was as important as his physical health in order to beat this virus. She felt he didn't quite seem like himself yet.

Then she received a text the next morning that turned it all around. 5:30 a.m.: **Morning, love.**♥

That simple text message made her feel like her husband was back. They FaceTimed. It was the first time in a long time that they got to spend more than a few minutes on the phone together—two hours. Rene was too weak to talk much, so it was mostly a one-way conversation. Tracy played him worship songs, talked to him, and sang. He fell asleep. She rested her head on the bed and stared at him. It was the best two hours.

Eventually Rene would become strong enough to go home. He would slowly recover and return to his family. He is living proof that even a pandemic cannot cancel faith.

Rene and Tracy Segura reside in Barrie, Ontario, with their three children and are the owners of Creative Bean Café. You can find them @creativebeanbarrie.

MOURNING IS NOT CANCELLED

By Catherine Kenwell

TODAY I ATTENDED A FUNERAL. And I was heartbroken I wasn't there.

See, my bestie's mom died earlier this week.

Less than twenty-four hours previously, my Aunt Betty—the last of my Mom's four sisters—passed away in long-term care.

Two women. One a whispered cremation, with no service. The other, a COVID-19 funeral with no congregation allowed.

Between the two of them, Betty and Vida earned almost 200 years here on earth. These women—mothers, daughters, sisters—grew up during the 1930s Depression and were young ladies during World War II. They witnessed the Red Scare, Elvis Presley, the first man on the moon . . . they raised their Baby Boomer children during the optimism of the 1960s and watched as they began to leave their nests in the 1970s and 80s.

And now, they have passed away during yet another significant cultural transformation. We can still recall where we were when Neil Armstrong took that first moon step, or what we were doing when we heard Kobe Bryant's plane crashed. But it will be difficult to recall where we were or what we were doing during this time . . . because our lives are largely on hold and one day seems to run into the next. And yet we mourn, and our days go by.

While we're obsessed with the latest COVID-19 numbers, life—and death—go on. Living with a loved one's passing is tough at any time, but when physical distancing restricts celebrations—including celebrations of life—we feel discombobulated and alone. Without formalities and rituals, many of us are not certain how to mourn . . . without human contact, we may feel guilt and love and dismay and all kinds of conflicting emotions. Because without our bodies to lead us to the hugs and comfort and physical touch we yearn for, our minds scatter. We feel sorrow and care, but we are unable to express our emotions physically.

My bestie's mom's funeral service was live-streamed; there were six family members and one officiant present. In the room.

What is that room called? A funeral *parlour*? That feels like such an antiquated term, a word that brings forth imagery of wooing suitors and the reading of telegrams from afar. I think of classic movies and women and men outfitted in their finery. Parlour. It is where we pay our respects. But not right now.

I wanted to pay my respects to a woman who was often like a second mom to me. I ached to congregate with others who were full of both deep sorrow and muted joy in our thoughts of a life well lived.

And I wanted to be close to the little girl I first met in grade two; the girl who was my bestie all along, the teen who fell in love and married her sweetheart, the woman who gave birth to a wonderful daughter who is so much like her mom. My maid of honor. My crazy-hair twin. The beautiful being who rallied the troops when she feared for my well-being. My soul sister.

So I showered and dressed and did my hair. I donned a dress. I put on lipstick. The everyday rituals that have eroded since March. I felt like there was comfort in maintaining a proper decorum, as if dressing in my Sunday best would somehow offer a sense of ceremony and perhaps, when it was over, a little closure.

Although I wonder if people even dress in Sunday best anymore . . . lately, my Sunday wardrobe has been whatever I wore to bed on Saturday night, sometimes followed by dirty jeans, a hoodie, and rubber boots if I decide to work in the garden.

So many trains of thought running through my brain. My brain is the broken engine that could; even when the tracks are flooded, I keep pushing along.

Parlour, decorum, Sunday best . . . my mind meanderings fell away when the officiant took to the podium.

Her words . . . were lovely, delivered in a compassionate, measured voice.

I gazed first at the casket and then at the back of my bestie's head as she sat in the front row, holding her grandson close.

The back of my bestie's head. How familiar it was, how tender and vulnerable and strong. I wanted to place my hand there, to somehow heal her, to absorb and thus lessen her pain. Involuntarily my hand reached for the computer monitor. It was the best I could do. I prayed she could feel it. And I wept.

When the parlour six stood, I stood. When they prayed, I bowed my head.

Their surroundings were stark and impersonal, made even more so by the absence of friends and family. Conversely, I sat alone, rod-straight in my office chair, surrounded by treasures— my books, my found objects, my comfort.

I learned that this mom I loved has comfort in her casket; a sweater, belonging to her mother—my bestie's grandmother— that she had worn almost every day for the past few months. The sweater was V's treasure, her found object, her comfort.

That simple gesture, that inclusion, was comfort indeed. From afar, I imagined the softness of that sweater, the gentleness with which it was placed alongside the body.

As the recessional song played, funeral staff moved forward to remove the casket. I am friends with one of them. "Matt," I whispered. "Take good care of her. She's my bestie's mom."

JOKES ARE NOT CANCELLED

BY HEATHER DOWN WITH JAMIE ANDERSON

SAM PICKED UP THE PHONE as he did most days and dialed 1-877-JOY-4ALL. The voice on the other end answered, "Hi, and thank you for calling Joy 4 All. We know that isolation is difficult, and we want to keep you company with voices of children and youth from your community. We are a youth-run project, and we want to bring you a healthy dose of joy each day of the week. You can select options from our menu to hear stories, jokes, and more. Please know that we send our warm wishes and can't wait to see you all again. Take care and stay safe."

Sam shifted the phone receiver to his other ear. Next came the options: "Please listen carefully to the following options to select what you would like to hear. Dial one to listen to jokes of the day. Dial two to hear today's story. Dial three for the poem of the day. Dial four for the daily dose of kindness and dial five to listen and learn."

Sam paused for a moment before making his decision.

EVER ACTIVE SCHOOLS IS AN organization in Alberta that works province-wide to support healthy schools and communities through physical literacy and mental well-being. The realm of their work centres more around physical and health education, but Ever Active Schools partnered with the City of Calgary, the Calgary Board of Education, and Calgary Public Libraries to offer a program called Recreational Leadership. This program, taught by Jamie Anderson, fills a gap by providing experiential learning opportunities in the area of human services, affording high school students, grades ten through twelve, a chance to work with children and youth.

Before the pandemic hit Alberta, the group of twenty-one students would meet at Calgary's downtown Central Public library. The students would come from all over the city to work together through a number of different courses and gain work experience, allowing them to build a portfolio and a resumé based on life experience. A big part of gaining that experience was through volunteering.

This year, the class was going to offer kids' programming for the library during break. They planned to create activities based on themes, offering arts and crafts and physical activity led by the high school students.

However, these plans were abruptly cancelled because of the public health measures being put in place. This group was faced with a challenge. They had to adapt.

The students were really looking forward to volunteering and were disappointed. Some of them voiced their displeasure. "I still want to volunteer."

"What are we going to do?" questioned another.

"How can we still be involved in something?"

That is when a seed for an idea was planted. They had heard there was a pretty significant need among a lot of seniors. In Calgary, many seniors were hard hit by COVID-19, and long-term care homes were on lockdown. With this added isolation and possible separation from emotional supports, it could have an impact on their mental health. What if the Recreational Leadership class were to provide something that brought joy to a sector who might otherwise be alone? And, to take it one step further, what if children and youth could provide that content? They also knew that real-time conversations were beyond the scope of what the class could provide. The students had to work within the reality of the size and reach of their program.

To connect these two groups—seniors and youth—project Joy 4 All was born. The class would set up a phone line where people could call in. Callers could hear jokes or stories to cheer them up, and the content would be contributed by young people who could either record their messages or email in written content for the students to record.

The class chose a phone line as the best means to offer this content because, especially for seniors, that choice seemed to have the least number of barriers to access. Not all long-term care homes had a plethora of readily accessible computers and devices. A good old-fashioned phone line would do the trick!

It was a big project with the extra challenge of being completed while in isolation. The students were divided into subgroups with different responsibilities: website, content, recording, posters, social media, logistics, and scheduling. They had to use video chats and emails to get the work done.

But they achieved their goal and the phone line was very successful, with as many as 4,000 call-ins per week. Teacher Jamie Anderson witnessed another phenomenon, one he couldn't have predicted. Even though his students were now physically separated, he saw individual students grow closer connections to each other and to the class as a whole as the excitement about being involved with such a unique project grew and gained momentum.

SAM WAS IN THE MOOD for some jokes, so he pressed option one.

"Hello, my name is Geri-Lynn, and I'm here to share some humour with you. Today's jokes come to us from Ariel. What did the couch say to the other couch at the other side of the room?" A light pause followed. "We are 'sofa' apart . . ."

Sam chuckled. The joke was so bad it was good. And in that moment, he didn't feel quite so alone.

Jamie Anderson is a passionate educator, having taught grades five through twelve over the eight years of his teaching career. He works with Ever Active Schools and the City of Calgary to deliver the Recreational Leadership program to students in the Calgary Board of Education, in partnership with Calgary Public Libraries. Outside of the classroom, he is entering the PhD program at the University of Calgary, with research interests in critical social justice in Alberta's schools.

BREAD DELIVERY IS NOT CANCELLED

BY SHELLEY HOFER WITH NIKKI GLAHN

WHEN I LOOK OUT MY front window, the view is essentially the same every day. Little things like seasonal changes or the odd curious skunk waddling along my front stoop keep it interesting. My dog, Loki, loves to sit on the couch and stare out the window.

When I look out my front window, it's hard to tell that there's a pandemic happening. That hundreds of thousands of people are getting sick. And some are dying. On this side of the pane, we are warm, healthy, and safe. Our bellies are full, and we have a slew of entertainment choices, a lovable dog to snuggle with and walk, and a basketball net to keep us distracted.

I gaze out my window and behold the sweet sight of my friend Nikki! She came by to pop two carefully wrapped loaves of freshly baked bread in my mailbox for me to pass along to my two senior neighbours. Someone had connected her with someone who knew another someone who was baking dozens of loaves of bread each day for seniors who might not have a fresh loaf of bread on their table.

We are being asked to practise physical distancing. It's as much for our own safety as for those we love and cannot be near. I can't hug my friend. But despite the distance between us, it feels like the world has gotten smaller. We are more disconnected than ever, yet I'm feeling even more of a connection to this beautiful community we get to live in. Because of Nikki Glahn.

Nikki waves at my window, shows her radiant smile, and bounces back to her jeep with an energy I've always admired. She's a connector, a conduit of good energy. She's the glue, the strength, and the power behind community. She embodies humanity and compassion without even knowing it. She's the stuff that makes what feels like a wild-and-crazy-off-kilter-tilt-a-whirl-world-in-a-pandemic slow-w-w-w down and feel like something bearable. She's the magnetism that makes the world go around.

I gulp back a bit of a sob. I miss her physical presence. And now I know why.

You know the saying from our beloved Mr. Rogers? "When I was a boy and I would see scary things in the news, my mother would say to me, look for the helpers. You will always find people who are helping." Nikki is the helper. Even when there isn't a pandemic, she's connecting people in our community, enthusiastically supporting local entrepreneurs, making meals for others and So. Much. More. She steps in to help before it's needed. She does it quietly and humbly.

Just a few short weeks ago, she knew she needed to help. And on March 14, 2020, at 9 p.m., she created a simple Facebook group hoping to connect those with needs to the helpers. Today, Barrie Families Unite has more than 9,000 members. There are four tireless administrators and sixteen enthusiastic moderators, all volunteers, all with their own delightful sense of humour and complementary skills—all recruited, trained, and inspired by Nikki.

Every single amazing quality that Nikki possesses is built into the page. Kindness, respect, generosity, charity, compassion, and a beautiful sense of humour. Within Facebook groups, you can create topics to keep posts organized and easily found. The most celebrated topic category on the BFU page is called "Yay!! Completed Cases." There are over 400 posts (and counting) in that topic. And a post only gets moved into this illustrious category when a need has been met. Over 400 people helped. There is a sense of pride in this topic. Groceries being delivered to those who need them most, questions answered, support given, meals delivered to a senior, even just letting someone know they're doing a good job.

Moderator Holly was touched by a post: "There was an anonymous post for a lady in need of a little food, another lady stepped up to buy it and drop it off, and even made sure she added something sweet that she wanted. The very next week, the same lady doing the buy contacted me to see if she needed a little more, the

Mom did and she got it for her and dropped it off again, I just thought that was so sweet!"

There have been over 200,000 posts, comments, and reactions. Every single one of them touched, seen, or shared by Nikki, the BFU team, and group members from our beautiful city. Our city council members, our mayor, and even national sources have given accolades for the tremendous support the group has inspired, for sharing important information, and for making our community feel like an amazing place to live. But it hasn't been without a touch of criticism. Nikki and the team take a firm stance on keeping the page debate-free and judgment-free, despite some pushback of some wanting to air their opinions. Nikki simply says, "If you'd like to debate, there are many other places to do it." This group is about helping people in a space that is non-judgmental and safe. People don't reach out when there is judgment.

Moderator Linda hasn't met the BFU team in person but feels a kinship with the people behind the scenes. "When the team is on a roll and connected, we can converse with gifs! So fun!" You might not know how heavy things can get in the back end of a page. We all recognize that people may be struggling, and many fires are put out before they become issues. The team sticks together solving issues, and they support each other.

The Facebook group shares an amazing amount of humour through memes and the camaraderie of connecting on topics we are all going through—like online learning and how to reinvent Easter when you don't have supplies. We are figuring this out. Easter isn't cancelled. Fun isn't cancelled. Creativity isn't cancelled. This is Nikki to a T. And she's reliable. Always. So is the way the team shares information on the page. You know it's reliably sourced and always with the intention of being helpful.

We take care of each other. Our community takes care of each other.

Moderator Karen remembers a post about a pregnant woman who expressed anxiety and fear about attending her doctor's appointment the next day. Another member posted a description about what to expect, what they're doing to keep everyone safe at the OB/GYN office—just to help calm her fears.

Nikki jumps in when called. She isn't afraid to learn something new. She's stretching her heart muscles and handling the negative comments with a sense of compassion far beyond what one might expect when being in the middle of a pandemic.

Moderator Carolina says she "loves seeing how fast people jump to offer help. It's amazing, really. It almost feels like some people are on the lookout to see where they can help and instantly offer. That leaves me in awe every time!"

I look out my window and Nikki is still in her Jeep. I'm guessing she's connecting with the next location she wishes to drop more bread off to. The David Busby Centre? The Women & Children's Shelter? The tired front-line staff at RVH? Another senior living alone and unable to make ends meet? Then she drives off, ready to check off another task on her beautiful list of helping people feel like the important community members they are.

Nikki messages me one day and says, I have had soooo many moments during this process to pick just one! I cried today as I left a house where I had just dropped 150 bottles of protein drinks and a small bag of Easter goodies for the young girl in the household. I mean, within an hour of me putting up an anonymous post I had $125-worth of donations plus two cases of protein drinks from Costco. People who don't even have all that much extra right now . . . giving what they could. People looking out for their neighbours and seniors. People LOVING up our front-line workers. People painting rocks with inspiring words and scattering them in the neighbourhood for others to 'stumble' upon. The lady who drove up from Toronto to deliver 12 loaves of bread, 40 pastries, and a bag full of baguettes. It just makes my heart burst with pride in humanity.

I wanted to write something prolific and inspiring with an amazing take-home, gut-punching lesson that would obviously follow the story of a community member who helped during a global pandemic. Because the subject of this story is a person who IS all of those things. Words aren't always easy to express, and I know

Nikki would deflect and say something like "It's a team effort!" So Nikki, thank you for putting in motion a space for everyone to feel welcome, needed, helpful, kind, generous, and safe.

She's busy but still takes the time to text me and remind me that "I'm enough." This is her superpower. She gives you complete permission to be exactly who you are. She's the holder of the space. She's the love that heals. She's the connection to the person who knows the person who made the life-saving bread who often goes unnoticed. She is the definition of altruistic. She's the epitome of kindness. And community. Nikki, you're enough.

I look out my window as she drives away and realize nothing could cancel the things that make Nikki *Nikki*—not even a global pandemic. It doesn't matter where she goes, she leaves behind love, community, and possibility. She leaves behind hope that we will all move through this . . . together.

Shelley Hofer and Nikki Glahn reside in the same Ontario city and have been friends throughout the past decade. Shelley is grateful that Nikki reminds her of her own courage when things are uncomfortable.

This morning at the grocery store, I said "sorry" to someone because I might've accidentally stepped within their 2 metre #SocialDistancing radius for a second, and I then felt a moment of Canadian pride for discovering a new opportunity to apologize to total strangers.

Suresh Singaratnam is a trumpeter and composer based in Mississauga, Ontario. Learn more about Suresh and his music at whoissuresh.com and icantihavetopractice.com.

BAKING IS NOT CANCELLED

BY HEATHER DOWN WITH MARY JANET MACDONALD

THE SOOTHING TONES OF SIXTY-SOMETHING Mary Janet MacDonald's singsong voice crooned through her Facebook Live feed: "Hello, everybody. I've never done this before, and I just want to welcome each and every one of you to my Cape Breton kitchen. And I want to say hi to my own children . . ."

Mary Janet smiled and waved to the camera on her phone as she named off all seven of her children: Tammy, Brennan, Margie, Gordie, Kelly, Krista, and Mitchell. She was teaching the nation—and beyond—how to bake her much-loved cinnamon rolls.

The maternal nature was palpable, even seen through the pixels on a screen. Mary Janet just felt like anybody's ideal grandmother, whether you were related to her or not.

Maybe that is because Mary Janet is no stranger to needing a mother. Kindness trumps blood. She lost her own mother when she was three years old. Her mother was very sick, and Mary Janet was raised by her grand-aunt from the age of one. Her three older school-aged siblings stayed with her father. However, she and her younger brother were taken in by two different grand-aunts. Mary Janet and her four siblings all lived in the same community but were divided between three separate homes.

Mary Janet's new mother was already the mother of six. Mary Janet considered this to be an amazing home, and the woman who raised her *was* Mama, and the six other children *were* her siblings. She is deeply grateful for all the little graces that have come her way throughout her lifetime. In addition to her immediate siblings, whom she has grown closer to as they entered into adulthood, she also has six other beautiful siblings to call her own.

One of her "sisters," Minnie, is mother to Canada's adored fiddle player, Natalie MacMaster. But that certainly isn't Mary Janet's only brush with Canadian musical royalty. Her own son, Mitch MacDonald, placed second in the 2008 season of *Canadian Idol*. Mitch, or Mitchell, as Mary Janet *always* calls him, is the baby and the only one of her children who still resides on Cape Breton Island. He lives with his own family only a few doors down the road.

Despite all her children being scattered across Canada, the family members are very close. Even though they have found themselves spread out, they make spending time together work with social media and Zoom.

Once the lockdown hit, a conversation began on Facebook. Daughter Margie, a teacher in Fort McMurray, was living in her condo and unable to go to work. She was wondering what sorts of things they could do to pass the time.

A few years ago, Margie had spearheaded a photo challenge on Facebook based on themes, and it was a lot of fun. This memory was a springboard to another idea: Mom, why don't you just do a live video and make something like our family favourite cinnamon rolls or Grandma's molasses cookies? Or something like that?

Mary Janet replied: Yeah. I could do that. That would be fun . . . but how do we do that?

Mary Janet didn't really have a click or a clue how to do a Facebook Live video.

But the idea of teaching appealed to her. In fact, it was something she had a lot of experience with, and to be honest, missed. For over thirty years, she had taught Cape Breton–style stepdancing. It had taken her to many places: Denmark, Scotland, the United States, and across Canada. She had taught most of the children in their community to step-dance. She had also instructed with 4H and loved to teach her own children how to do things.

She thought, *I could teach people how to make these cinnamon rolls from scratch.* Although there were lots of inexperienced bakers out there, Mary Janet was confident she could break down the steps and share her recipe with everybody. She wanted people to know that baking wasn't a scary thing, and she wanted to show people that they *could* bake bread—and they could make cinnamon rolls, even.

So Mary Janet set up her phone on a Sunday afternoon and decided to offer a baking lesson. She figured she would pretend she was just talking to one person and walk them through the baking process. Throughout the video, her kids kept texting, asking her if she remembered to say this or to do that . . . or to mention the temperature of the oven! Celtic music played softly in the background, and her instructions were sometimes reinforced with the sound of their ringing landline.

It wasn't a slickly produced HGTV cooking show; it was something better—it was real. And it resonated with a country in turmoil. A country looking for something calming and familiar, like Grandma's Cape Breton kitchen.

Referring to Cape Breton, Mary Janet quipped, "Margie's boyfriend calls it the carb coast. I am a perfect example of that."

She punctuated her point with the cutest of self-deprecating giggles.

When it was all over and done with, Margie called. "Mom, do you know how many people were tuned in to that?"

"No," Mary Janet replied.

"Over 500 people watched your live video!"

Mary Janet nearly keeled over, she was so surprised. She figured friends and family might enjoy her debut video, but she had no idea its reach would spread.

As the video remained online, the views climbed exponentially. The Facebook page Tunes and Wooden Spoons was officially born and to date has over 30,000 followers.

Mary Janet was both humbled and shocked by the number of kind messages she received. One young woman from across the country had lost the inclination to return to her beloved baking after an accident that had left her with a traumatic brain injury. She told Mary Janet that she watched her video over and over again, bringing her such a sense of calm. It was just what she needed on that day to bring kindness and goodness to this period of fear we were all going through.

Mary Janet had created more than just cinnamon rolls. She had created soul food—feeding the bellies and hearts of people across our nation. And that kind of food will sustain us for a very long time.

MJ's Cinnamon Rolls

This one is certainly a family favourite.
Here is the recipe:
4 cups flour
6 tsp baking powder
2 tsp salt
2 heaping tbsp white sugar

Mix together and then add 1/2 cup shortening (or butter). Mix well with hands (the old-fashioned way) until all the shortening is incorporated. Make a well in the centre and add 2 cups milk; using a fork, blend the flour into the milk and stir just enough until there is no flour residue. Place dough on a floured surface and sprinkle a bit of flour on top as well. Form the dough into a ball without working it too much but try to have a smooth surface on top. Roll out into a sort of rectangle to about 1/4 to 1/2 inch. Using about 1/2 cup of softened butter or margarine, spread it all over the surface right to the edges. Sprinkle with about 1 1/2 cups brown sugar and spread the sugar right to the edges. Sprinkle cinnamon over the whole surface. Roll up like a jelly roll and slice each circle about 3/4 inch thick. Place on a parchment-lined cookie sheet (I use a stoneware bar pan). You should be able to have about 15 cinnamon rolls on the cookie sheet, each one slightly touching each other. Bake in a 425-degree oven for 15 to 18 minutes. (If using a metal cookie sheet, double up on the cookie sheets as the cinnamon rolls tend to scorch easily on regular metal baking sheets. Watch carefully.)

When out of the oven, let cool for about 5 minutes and add a swipe of frosting: 3 tbsp soft butter or margarine, 2 tsp vanilla, about 2 cups icing sugar, and a little splash of milk. Start to mix and if too dry, add a tiny bit more milk until you have the consistency of peanut butter.

Author's note: After interviewing Mary Janet, she was kind enough to put a call-out for me so I could receive people's reactions directly. At first, I was going to try to incorporate them into the narrative, but these voices, in their own words, do a much better job.

Hi Heather,

Tonight I baked a butterscotch pie from scratch. I had ensured to buy the ingredients on my weekly grocery list in the COVID-19 environment. I am not a baker, but this lady, MJ, well she just brings some downhome back into life through a phone—and my wife's favourite dessert is butterscotch pie.

After five weeks at home, my kids begged me this morning to just take them for a drive so they could sit in the car and see something different. The day moved from one thing to the next, and it didn't look like I was going to get to the pie today. In fact, I missed the live lesson! I was resolved to do it at some other time.

It was a call from a family friend that sent me reeling. I was informed that a fellow hockey coach had just lost his wife, an RCMP officer, to a shooter on a rampage that led to the death of twenty-two innocent people. I was dazed throughout the evening, checking social media, and hurting with the rest of the province. At some point, I decided that I must do something else to help get my mind off what was eating away at me. I turned to MJ and her Tunes and Wooden spoons. I would make a pie.

That was odd for me. I'm a singer and a songwriter, so music would be the obvious choice—but tonight MJ helped take my mind off the stress of the COVID-19 pandemic and questioning why someone would have a complete disregard for human life. For about an hour or so, I took a break and made my wife and kids a butterscotch pie. It may not sound like much, but it helped me cope with the news of one of our community members, and the twenty-one others that lost their lives in an already stressful time. The music stopped today when Constable Heidi Stevenson was taken, but some simple ingredients, and a kind soul from a Cape Breton kitchen, provided some respite for at least one person today . . . despite the fact that I messed up the first one and had to start over.

– Jason Price

Hi Heather,

I've been following Tunes and Wooden Spoons every week. I first saw it on Facebook from the news article. There were two or three videos posted by then, and I stayed up until 3:00 a.m. that night just watching them. I love watching cooking shows, but this was so good because it was just a real unrehearsed mom showing her family recipes. It's nice to have something else to think about rather than the news.

I made the cinnamon buns and they were so amazing and easy!

I'm a dental hygienist off work and a single mother of an amazing thirteen-year-old daughter. I try to not go out very often, so I love her recipes because most of it is stuff you have at home anyway if you do any cooking at all.

– Jennifer Lagacy-Shaw, Hawkins Corner, New Brunswick

Hello Heather,

I understand you are interested in receiving little anecdotes of positive things that have arisen from this COVID-19 isolation. I stumbled across Tunes and Wooden Spoons on Facebook recently. I enjoyed watching one of Mary Janet's videos. The next day, my mother, who is ninety-five years young, moved in to stay with us during this isolation. She lives independently but has found it very lonely and isolating because her children and grandchildren aren't able to visit as they don't want to risk her health.

So I am introducing her to technology, and she is able to communicate with her other children, grandchildren, and great-grandchildren through FaceTime. Today I told her about this lovely lady at Tunes and Wooden Spoons who we were going to bake pies with. We set up the iPad and baked apple pie with her, and my mom was thrilled. My mom was amazed by this technology and how we could bake with this lady in Nova Scotia. For me, it was a wonderful memory to have with my mom in her ninety-fifth year. And believe me, we did definitely enjoy this apple pie together!!

– Arlene Anderson along with my mother, Mabel Senchuk, Winnipeg, Manitoba

Good afternoon Heather!

With these crazy times right now, it is easy to get lost and feel anxiety, especially for those who suffer from anxiety on a regular basis. Well, when I found Mary Janet, it was like a blessing, truly. She's funny, cute, inspiring, down to earth, calming, and so lovely to watch and listen to. I can't get enough of her stories!

I look forward to watching her every Sunday live. Just to get lost a little and take my mind off everything, even just for an hour. I always feel calmer and happy after watching her, and I believe she has touched a lot of people, and she probably doesn't even realize how many.

She has seven children, but after this I am sure she has many more now!

– Maria Breen

Hi Heather,

Just watched Mary Janet's pie video. I discovered MJ a couple of weeks ago and love watching her—and I love to bake. She is such a lovely lady. My husband and I are originally from Cape Breton and now that we are retired, we spend quite a bit of time on our property there.

We have lived in Alberta for thirty-eight years. Not being able to go back to see our family is a hardship right now, but baking does help pass the time. Many of MJ's recipes are the recipes my mother frequently baked (she was a wonderful baker as well). Mary Janet's videos are a real gift as her recipes bring back fond memories of Mom, and I now have some of the recipes I never had a chance to get from Mom! Also spending time with MJ virtually is like visiting with an old friend. Just love it!

– Janet MacDonald Alexander

Hello,

Being a Cape Bretoner living in the wild west for the past thirteen years has been fulfilling and lonely on any good day. With the way the world has now changed over the last five weeks and the uncertainties that I feel for our children, I worry deeply. We miss our family and friend connection, but I also find myself missing the far away connection.

And here enters Mary Janet MacDonald, or as our family has dubbed her, the Facebook nanny. She's everything we miss: the baking and tea times with our nannies, grandmothers, and mothers who are far from us—or even right down the road but we cannot see. She brings her Cape Breton soul into our kitchen from 5,000 kilometres away and makes us feel like we're part of the family. But being from Cape Breton, you already are part of the family, even if you don't know it.

Mary Janet MacDonald in my mind is the definition of what Cape Breton is, an open kitchen and a fresh pot of tea. Home!

– V Bernard

Hello Heather!

I'm writing to you from Oakdale, Connecticut, USA, and want to let you know how much joy Mary Janet MacDonald has brought to me here in the Tri-State epicentre of COVID-19 in the United States.

As a mother with two stepdaughters working in medicine who are trying desperately to stop the spread of COVID-19—and who are searching for a treatment—Mary Janet has been a breath of fresh air for me and someone to ease my worries.

Our youngest daughter, a scientist in Boston, Massachusetts, is frantically working on finding a vaccination for COVID-19. She has spent many, many hours trying to learn how the virus mutates.

Our eldest daughter is in charge of Infectious Disease in two of our local hospitals, and she has been putting in countless hours to try to keep all those in our hospitals safe, and more importantly, alive.

My husband, the girls' father, and I are also "essential workers," working every day during this pandemic. Our daughters' safety is always on our minds. When I stumbled upon Mary Janet's page, she instantly calmed my worries with her friendly smile and soothing music playing while she cooked.

I cannot express enough all that Mary Janet has done for me. Her recipes, music, and videos have been a Godsend to my inner peace. Not to mention my husband enjoying someone from Cape Breton—considering that his family were founding fathers of Mahone Bay, Nova Scotia.

– Davilee Deal

Hello Heather,

We are a group of ten ladies in Dartmouth, who have been so inspired by Mary Janet. We have known each other for nearly forty years. We have had many gatherings over the past years, sharing happiness and heartbreak and, of course, many meals with tea and treats.

Mary Janet has come along at a time when we needed her most. We have not been able to physically socialize because of the coronavirus, so we have been chatting via social media. We chat usually two times a week and try to come up with creative ways to make it interesting. After watching Mary Janet, I was inspired not only by her baking but also by the fact that she encouraged everyone to use their good China teacups for their tea. I have beautiful china teacups my grandmother left me, so I decided to put them in a prominent place in my dining room instead of at the back of a cupboard in the kitchen.

Our last chat was a trivia chat along with our favourite China teacup and a Mary Janet cookie. When we are able to get back together for a real gab session, we have decided to have a Mary Janet tea!

– Elizabeth Corkery

Mary Janet MacDonald is the proud mother of seven wonderful children and lives in Port Hood, Nova Scotia. To learn more about her or to check out her videos on Facebook, YouTube, or Instagram, look for @TunesAndWoodenSpoons.

Photo credit: Matthew Heneghan

BEAUTY IS NOT CANCELLED

BY MATTHEW HENEGHAN

*For in much wisdom is much grief: and he that increaseth
knowledge increaseth sorrow.*
– Ecclesiastes 1:18

I WOULDN'T CONSIDER MYSELF A wise man. Neither do I boast the gift of intellect. I do, however, hold knowledge of a few things, the most notable being grief. My childhood left a mark on me—both physically and otherwise . . . But my grief was also recent.

December 2019 was a month designed to be joyous and unique from all others. Whether you celebrate, recognize, condone, or understand Christmas, here in the west, come December, it is undeniable that things change. Hyperconsumerism followed by get-togethers and city streets replete with festive glow. Things are just different.

It was evening time when the call came in. I had been sitting on my couch, getting lost in the vast, sand-speckled pages of a good book. It was interrupted by sombre news from home. My sister had called to inform me that our other sister, Lisa, was in a bad way. Being the youngest of five, I am closest to Lisa in age, and we spent a lot of time together growing up. But, arguably, not enough.

My sister Lisa had lived a hard life. She battled demons of the past and sinister vices in the present. Something I can relate to. By the time December of 2019 had rolled around, I had been sober for 487 days after having floundered in a bottle for almost ten years.

"Hey, Sandra. What's up?"

"Matthew . . . it's Lisa. She's talking about killing herself."

I sat back and fell victim to the weight of my sister's words. Suicide is a touchy subject in our family. Our mother had been murdered by a poisoned mind a mere two years before. Her note is still fresh behind my eyes. Even thinking about it, the air becomes thin. Almost . . . impossible. The air becomes poison and I cannot breathe.

As my sister continued, I felt my chest tighten. Not again. This can't happen again so soon . . . I had to fight against myself and demand that I remain in the present. My mind was racing, and my palms were beginning to sweat. We finished talking, and I proceeded to call Lisa right away. The phone rang far too many times for my liking, but eventually my ears were greeted by my sister's cheerless mezzo.

"Hi."

"Hey, Lisa . . . How ya doing?"

"Fine."

"Yeah . . . ? You don't sound all that fine . . ."

"No. I'm fine, Matty."

We went back and forth like this for a bit. A chess game of oration, if you will. I realized I just had to come right out with it, so I approached the topic very gently. She informed me that she was sad. And that she was sad of always being sad. Hearing that was . . . sad. Perhaps made even more so by the fact of how relatable it was.

We talked about Mum. She told me how much she missed her. How angry she was at her for dying the way she did. For taking away any more years that we could have had with her. Growing up, we all lived with a constant worry that our mother could die at any moment. This was born from the fact that our mum battled cancer on and off for a great number of years. Eventually, it was sadness that killed her. She beat cancer. Life beat her.

My sister was taken to the hospital by the police. Over the following days and weeks, she and I held nightly phone conversations. She lived across the country from me, so phone calls were the best we could do.

I was hopeful that things were getting better. We even shared a few untamed bits of laughter. A genuine Lisa laugh . . . that's as rare an artifact as you will ever encounter.

December 15, 6:44 p.m. For the duration of forty-two minutes and twenty-six seconds, I spoke to my sister. We spoke playfully and earnestly with one another. I told her I was going to make some dinner and that I would call her later that night. I never did. I fell asleep. And now, I wish more than anything that I hadn't. That fifteenth day of December was the last time I would ever speak to my big sis. I tried to call her several times in the ensuing weeks, but I never got through.

On January 5, 2020, a meagre five days into the new year, my sister was pronounced dead. She had been taken to the hospital the night prior after collapsing from shortness of breath. She was said to have died from sepsis. So, by way of definition, the very air she was begging for was poison. Dead from a broken heart and poisoned lungs.

Depression befell me insidiously after that day. Getting out of bed was nearly impossible. Breathing became a chore. Every inhalation hurt. Everything hurt. The air was poison. As it so often is when it comes to trauma and pain.

I was able to rid myself of the shackles of stagnation. Not all at once, but bit by bit, I began to breathe. Therapy and introspection acted as oxygenated relief for me. I still had my moments, sure. Times where my tears in the shower competed with the volume of falling water. But navigating the everyday beneath a heft of sadness is nothing new for me; as I have said, I hold some knowledge in loss . . . and as the big book says, in knowledge there is sorrow.

In an attempt to inject some colour and life back into my dreary existence, I bought a camera. I held belief—scratch that—I held *hope* that viewing the world through a window designed to capture beauty would force me to find some of it. And if I could capture it and freeze it, perhaps I could hold onto it.

I knew nothing of photography. Nothing outside of point and shoot. But I was excited to challenge myself. Drinking used to be the thing that took me away. Or so I had once thought. In reality, all it did was numb the world. A tempting proposition considering current life events. But that's a record I've played to the end far too many times before. I know where it goes . . . and it's not beautiful.

I began first with taking some simple snapshots around my apartment, building up the courage to hold this incredible moment-capturing device in public. Little did I know that being creative with my dwelling would become so important . . .

Several weeks after getting the camera, I was sitting in front of the TV, and I began to read the newsfeed scrolling at the bottom of the screen: NOVEL VIRUS DISCOVERED IN CHINA. EXPERTS FEAR IT IS ENDEMIC. One thing became clear in that moment: in China, the air was poison.

Fast-forward to present day; we are all inside now. The air is poison for us all. Well, kind of. It feels that way.

I can't help but find a duality in that statement and the consequence therein; trauma makes you feel as though breathing is impossible, even if just for a moment. But in that moment . . . poison. So we stay inside and isolate ourselves from the outside world. It feels safer that way. And now, with this, this invisible foe, we all hide. We all isolate. We are all left uneasy and uncertain. The air is poison.

Okay, we are not on total lockdown (thank goodness), but life has certainly changed. With that change, it has become even more important for me to find, capture, and hold beauty with that little window held to my eye. To peer through and phase out the rest of the world only to seize that one perfect moment in time. A freeze-frame where everything else ceases to matter, and all you are left with is a token of time etched from shards of light and glass. A gift from the gods, given through technology. There is no air in that photo. There are no narratives, no war, no death, and no pain . . . it is just . . . a still of perfect peace.

When I am my most sad, I now have snippets of when I was my most care-free to gaze upon. Because in the seconds before shutter meets shutter and aperture ingests light, I am totally and hypnotically grounded in the moment. The air above me may be poison, but the world around me is mesmeric and beautiful. I am not isolated. I am gifted to be alive.

I will continue to take pictures. Maybe if I store them in my heart, my sister and my mother—and all those I have lost—will see them, too. Through the window, I have found peace. One shot at a time. And sharing them . . . well, there is no isolation in sharing. I am not alone.

Matthew Heneghan is an avid podcaster and blogger who lives in Mississauga, Ontario. He is also the author of the mental health memoir A Medic's Mind. *To learn more about Matthew, visit amedicsmind.com.*

BOOK LAUNCHES ARE NOT CANCELLED

BY HEATHER DOWN WITH SÉAN MCCANN

SÉAN MCCANN, A FOUNDING MEMBER of Great Big Sea, bravely opened up about the clerical sexual abuse he encountered in his youth and the addictions he employed in attempting to drown the pain and trauma it caused. In 2013, he broke away from the band and pursued a course of truth, using music as his therapy. His new purpose landed on sharing his stories and songs of hope and recovery with those who needed it most.

If asked what keeps him sober, Séan will answer, "My higher power—Andrea."

Séan's wife, Andrea, found the strength to give Séan an ultimatum: get sober or she would move on. Séan chose his family. And, as difficult as it was, he pushed forward into a life of sobriety.

Public speaking led to an idea for another way to share his story, which resonated with so many. He and Andrea would write a book. The couple began the arduous task of penning their story from both their points of view, giving a 360-degree perspective of the role addiction plays within a family setting.

One Good Reason, a beautiful hardcover memoir punctuated with song lyrics and artwork, was scheduled to be released in April 2020. This was going to be Séan's focus for the next two years. They had partnered with the bookstore chain Indigo to do a national tour from St. John's to Vancouver, offering in-store events in almost every province. Séan would speak, sing, answer questions, and do signings in most urban centres. It took a lot of planning and work to coordinate this tour.

In addition, media appearances were confirmed with large networks, and national TV shows were booked. Sharing his story was something Séan was passionate and excited about doing. When rumblings of COVID-19 began in the beginning of 2020, no one really considered that the country would shut down like it did. Even to the last minute, everyone involved was still talking about the tour. Suddenly, it was all gone, and Séan and Andrea had no backup plan whatsoever.

They assumed this meant the release of the book would now be delayed, possibly to the fall. However, after talking to people in the business, and on the recommendation of the publisher, the book would go forward as planned. The thought was this was the right book for the times. It was a helpful, hopeful message, and people would benefit from it. This title might reach a lot of people regardless of a cancelled tour.

"Okay, let's put the book out," Séan said to Andrea. Other than a few radio interviews, the major media outlets had dried up because of cancelled production. "What should we do?" he asked.

Something would be better than nothing, so they decided to pivot to online. Before livestream concerts were plentiful, the couple used Facebook Live to present a fourteen-day series. Séan chose the number fourteen because, at that time in Ontario, residents were told the quarantine would likely last fourteen days. Initially, Andrea was to produce the show and to watch comments while Séan performed. However, while sitting behind Séan, she was brought into the camera frame when he couldn't hear her directions and turned around to talk to her. "You're out now. You might as well be part of the show."

And part of the show she was. Every day at noon, they livestreamed an hour of entertainment and chatter. It became known as the SéAndrea Show.

Before the series was complete, they added a bonus date. On the fifteenth day, they would culminate the series with an online book launch on their page, followed by an online Indigo launch.

The SéAndrea Show was able to raise awareness about the upcoming book, and pre-orders were robust. A thousand books arrived on a pallet to their Ottawa-area home. Séan and Andrea had also taken orders directly from their own website, offering special personally signed copies. It was a big job, but they signed and shipped out most of the books during a frenzied weekend.

At first the publishing company was going to hold off on the release of the ebook version; however, they, too, had to pivot. Digital editions were published at the same time as the hardcover, allowing people to download the title immediately onto their devices without even stepping out of their homes.

Séan was not in a hurry to create an audio version. He thought he would release it for Christmas. But with the postponed tour, he has more time on his hands. Since he has a home studio, he could start recording right away. He has decided to record exclusive renditions of the songs in the book and add dramatic instrumental music to link chapters together. It certainly will be a very special and unique audiobook.

Although the physical tour was cancelled, quick thinking, ingenuity, and hard work were not, allowing a beautiful book to be released and enjoyed by many, proving that, in the end, even a virus can't silence a hopeful story.

Besides being a founding member of the band Great Big Sea, Séan McCann is a sought-after speaker and performer. And now, he can add author to his list of many accomplishments. His book One Good Reason *is available where books are sold. You can follow Séan @seanmccannsings.*

THE SIMPLE WAY HOME IS NOT CANCELLED

BY CHEYANNA KIDD

IF LOOKS COULD KILL, I'D be dead. My little daughter's eyes glare up at me as she sits on the floor. The intensity of her rage overflows from her eyes into large teardrops. Her mouth gapes open like a tiny seething ogre, and she shrieks at me: a pitchy, deafening lash of unfairness. I look down at the dusty black running shoe I had taken from her. It's my partner's shoe. She had been chewing on it. This makes me a monster, apparently. I suppose parenthood is understood only by those who live it.

I scoop up my snivelling one-year-old bundle of drool and fury, carrying her back to the red loveseat in the living room. Or perhaps one could argue it was in the dining room. Our compact apartment has the legroom of a Smart car. Maybe if I were her size, it would seem less confining. I sigh, using a cloth to wipe the mess of tears, drool, and snot off her face. Tiny hands fight against me. I plop her down on the floor, half wiped. She rubs her face and stares at her feet.

"You can't eat your dad's shoes," I say to her. She doesn't understand, but she's mad at me anyway. I don't blame her. We've been stuck inside for weeks now. Nothing seems fun anymore.

Originally, we were going to drive all the way out to grandma's house. The two-day journey takes us through cascades of mountains, sprawling cities, and waving grassland. The world feels bigger there, endless, even. It's a world of people; a world of outside. It's a world where a little girl can smell the rain on the wind and snuggle up in a circle of family by a glowing campfire. It's where every meal is hearty, warm, and always ready . . . And everyone can take turns playing with her. She's so happy there. She's free.

I feel like we're trapping her here.

This tiny apartment has become a prison not only to her, but to us as well; my partner and I are exhausted. We're lonely.

We're struggling to make ends meet. I feel like I'm falling down a secluded tunnel of timeless, meaningless, empty space . . . at a time when I need to be more present than ever. I'm so distant. I'm failing her.

Glancing black to reality, I try to hide the sadness that's weighing down my face. I try to ignore the invisible bars along the windows and forget how much I miss the outside hustling world. I look over at my little girl, who's already bumbling her way over to another unfolded basket of trouble. Her chubby legs cycle, slapping and pummelling the floor in an enthusiastically animated crawl. She is determination incarnated. She is undeniably mine.

With her eyes fixated on the alluring promise of grabbable new clothes, I reach out and grasp her leg. Her tiny fingers stretch to grab the hard-plastic rim but fall an inch too short. I pull her back toward me. Her frustration ignites upon the realization, and she sprawls out like a pancake in an attempt to cling to the floor. A livid banshee screech resonates in the small room. I pick her up awkwardly and sit her in my lap. After a moment, her anger fades into a blubbery mess of confusion and betrayal.

Her watery eyes meet mine, begging for an answer. I wish she could understand how she's compromised. I wish she could see that there's an epidemic outside, and I hope she somehow knows I'm trying my best. I smooth her wild wisps of hair and cocoon her in my arms. Perhaps she feels like we're trapping her here, too.

She wiggles uncooperatively. I sigh and let her squirm onto the floor as a stubbornly contorted lump. Almost immediately, she zooms to the coffee table and hoists herself upward, attempting to crawl up onto it like a fish venturing onto land for the first time. As her arms reach as far forward as she can possibly manage, I see what's about to happen; I quickly snag the towering glass full of milk and whisk it away to the kitchen counter. Her eyes follow me across the room.

I watch her plop back down onto the floor and look down at her feet. She slouches with an unusual lack of lustre and quietly pokes her sock, not even bothering to look back at me again. A soft, sullen wave slowly washes over the room. I stand there, immersed. In the rare moment of silence, my heart only drops further.

I look at the glass on the countertop, the glass that her little heart only wanted to play with. It's heavy, sturdy, perhaps thick enough to stand a chance against being broken. I dump the milk into the sink and rinse it. Then, gently, I set the empty glass on the end of the coffee table.

Her eyes dart up to it and then over to me. Awkwardly and unevenly, she makes sidesteps toward the glass again. It glimmers in the sunlight like a beacon in a quest, lighting up her face. I catch myself starting to smile a little.

Her hands clasp around the glass with the unbridled confidence of a man with a large truck. Mesmerized, she attempts to pick it up. It tips over, unsurprisingly, and she intentionally pushes it over the edge of the table; a loud bang resonates like a shotgun in my mind, but the glass itself is unbroken. It rolls heavily across the laminate flooring and hits the bottom of the fridge. She drops down to chase after it like an overexcited puppy, her hands smacking the floor with every crawling step.

I follow her, watching her grab the glass by the rim and thrash it around experimentally. I take it from her, swapping it out for a bright red plastic cup from the counter. Even though she has toys that are nearly identical, this one is a thousand times better: it's usually forbidden to play with. Her little voice babbles happily at me, accompanied by the random percussion of the cup bonking against the floor.

I can't help but smile, wondering if I can find anything else that might entertain her. I scour the kitchen and closets, finding odds and ends of unused supplies, unworn clothing, and estranged missing things. Satisfied with my heaping armload of hidden treasures, I dump it all into a clear bin in the middle of the living room.

Riding this wave of inspiration, I notice how tall the chairs and shelves are. I grab the thin fabric of a nearby sheet and unfold it in the air with a whip of my arm. As it flutters outward, my little girl looks up in awe. I tie the corners to high anchor points around the room, creating the base for a blanket fort. I find more blankets, some arguably too small, and weave a sturdy, tent-like network. It hangs in the air, suspended by furniture, shelving, gates, boxes, and broom poles. I slide the junk bin inside the patchwork fort and look around me. The balcony sunlight illuminates the back of the fabrics like a stained-glass window. Disney characters glow, large butterflies feel alive, and the ceiling swirls like *The Starry Night*.

A childish giggle announces the arrival of my daughter, who pitter-patters through the front of the fort. The excitement in her eyes is unmatched. Surrounded by beauty that feels bigger than ourselves, I finally understand the majesty of simple things. For a moment, I feel like I'm really a part of her world.

The rattle of a small child hitting a junk bin brings me back to the present. I laugh softly and lift her onto a pillow beside me, so she can watch. I tip the bin over, spilling a tidal wave of random things onto the floor between us: a whisk, a new longboard wheel, an old remote, a French to English dictionary, bracelets, frilly hats, mismatched lids, hairbrushes, wooden pieces, flyers, glowsticks, and more.

Before I know it, we've made towers of junk, shakable containers, a small corral of stuffed animals, and an entire corner dedicated to different kinds of snacks. I smile more genuinely than I have all week. I let her choose another book for me to read to her, and she helps me turn the pages. Well, she turns them backwards, but that's all right. I laugh and improvise a new story with her. She giggles at me.

As I turn another backwards page, it dawns on me: she's found her happiness in here with me. The world feels bigger in here . . . endless, even. It's a world where a little girl can make sounds like rain on the wind and snuggle up in her mom's lap by a pile of newly discovered treasure. It's where the snack corner is endless, yummy, and always ready . . . And I can spend all day playing with her. She's so happy here. She's free.

Maybe Grandma's house isn't so far away after all.

Cheyanna Kidd is a proud young mother, a 3D animation student, and an artist with autism. Born in Tisdale, Saskatchewan, she now lives in Kelowna, British Columbia, with her daughter and with her loving partner, Kurtis. With a passion for adventure, nature, and the mysteries of the universe, she is on a journey to leave a positive mark on the world.

STORYTELLING IS NOT CANCELLED

By Heather Down with David A. Robertson

DAVID A. ROBERTSON SEES HIS job as a writer as including human interaction, visiting people face to face, and scheduling appearances. He had to get creative to achieve this in an era of physical distancing. A member of the Norway House Cree First Nation, his eclectic body of work spans graphic novels to children's books to literary fiction. One common thread is that he always writes about Indigenous people in one form or another. He feels there is great value in storytelling in the process of reconciliation.

David's parents split when he was young, and he grew up in Winnipeg. Later, when his parents reconciled, he became more curious about the cultural things he missed while growing up separated from his Indigenous roots. This ignited a passion, and he began to reconnect in earnest.

Currently, David's day job is in First Nations education where he manages publishing and communications at the Manitoba First Nations Education Resource Centre. When mandates for social distancing and other measures kicked into place with COVID-19, he and his staff started reading literature on Facebook Live to support the community. He also saw other authors offering readings online.

David decided to utilize social media platforms to share his personal work as well. He had been scheduled to go to Germany, Vancouver, and Anaheim, and although travel was out of the question, storytelling was not. His motivation for sharing readings online was twofold: First, he wanted to continue to connect with people, provide readings, further storytelling, and answer questions. Second, he wanted to support teachers and parents. Even though parents were doing lots of things with their children at home, David saw this as an opportunity for them to take a little breather while their children interacted with his readings.

David was asked to do an event after the FOLD (Festival of Literary Diversity) in Brampton had to reinvent itself. Because of the lockdown, this festival run by J.L. Richardson, decided to offer readings and workshops via Zoom. David was able to host an event, but he didn't have to travel, and he enjoyed the experience.

David also made the decision to read his picture book *When We Were Alone* on Twitter. He really didn't know what to expect. He was pleasantly surprised that quite a few people tuned in, and people commented and asked questions while he was reading. He was able to save the video for replay, so folks continued to comment and message him long after the performance was over.

Although he admits it isn't quite the same as being in the same room with a crowd of people, it still gets the job done. Adaptation seems to be a necessity at this time. After all, even his son's hockey camp is being delivered online!

David A. Robertson is the author of numerous books for young readers including When We Were Alone, *which won the 2017 Governor General's Literary Award and was nominated for the TD Canadian Children's Literature Award.* Strangers, *the first book in his Reckoner trilogy, a young adult supernatural mystery, won the 2018 Michael Van Rooy Award for Genre Fiction (Manitoba Book Awards). A sought-after speaker and educator, Dave is a member of the Norway House Cree Nation and currently lives in Winnipeg.*

TWELVE-STEP PROGRAMS ARE NOT CANCELLED

BY NATALIE HARRIS

WHEN I WAS AT THE lowest point in my addiction, I would sit in a dark basement, alone in a corner. I would wear earplugs and try to sleep my life away. I would do anything it took to not have human connection. I hated people because in the early days of my post-traumatic stress disorder, they represented evil. I felt like an alien. I craved being alone. I craved silence. And at one point I craved death.

I am one of the lucky ones. I was fortunate enough to have the opportunity to go to a treatment centre for my addiction and PTSD in 2015, and it was there that I was introduced to twelve-step programs. I knew I had to participate in them to be successful in the program, but there was one factor about the meetings that made me cringe: at the door at every meeting, people were waiting to shake my hand. It meant I needed to have human contact. I despised the thought of it. It filled me with anxiety and anger. But I was so far from the dark corner in my basement where I could hide that I forced myself to slowly warm up to the idea of at least faking a smile and shaking their hands. *Ugh.*

Years have gone by now. Long ago are the days when I craved isolation. I still go to twelve-step meetings every week—well, I should say I used to go, until COVID-19 stopped them abruptly and isolation was mandated; oh, how the tables had turned. But with desperation, there comes adaptation, and over the last few weeks Zoom twelve-step meetings from many different fellowships have started. People battling the disease of addiction knew they needed to make this happen fast. It was life or death for many of us; without any human contact, our addict brain would start screaming at us. I have been told once that while I am sober my addiction is doing push-ups, just waiting for me to stop my recovery work. Waiting to start the wheels of obsession and craving with a vengeance. It wouldn't take long for relapses and deaths to occur if we didn't find fellowship somewhere.

The first few meetings were funny. People were getting used to the technology of Zoom and learning how to make a scene from *Tiger King* their background; I don't judge . . . I considered doing the same! But as the days went by and people settled in, a very common theme appeared in the shares, one of restlessness and irritability and the most dangerous theme of all—fear. People were afraid of the emotions being quarantined was causing them to feel. People were afraid of the urge to just quiet the madness with a drink or drug because "no one would even know." People were afraid to even say they were afraid—people with long-term sobriety finally started to share that they felt as if maybe they had been getting by on a powerful ego much more than they had realized. Now that they were left alone with their thoughts and emotions, relapse from years of sobriety was truly only an arm's-length away.

Luckily, we have learned in the program that the opposite of fear is faith. I remind myself of this a lot these days. Fear is the common heavy wet blanket on the planet these days, and unless faith pushes it aside to show that the sun is still shining, we will surely lose our way; and for people battling the disease of addiction that means possibly losing their lives. So I have been bringing the topic of fear and ego up in meetings lately to, of course, realize that I am never alone in my thinking; I am simply alone in my room.

Zoom twelve-step meetings are a paradox to me. They are happening because we are isolated, but they are also ending isolation for some who may never have had the ability to leave their homes and attend a meeting in the first place. People with disabilities and who live remotely can join large Zoom meetings for the first time. Yes, without a handshake at the door or any public gatherings happening, we seem so far away from one another. But the other day when I looked at where the people were from in a Zoom meeting (California, Alberta, Texas, Nova Scotia . . .), I realized that in a strange way we are now all much closer than we ever were before.

Humans are amazing (I'm happy to say that I generally like them nowadays). We adapt and do whatever we can to keep connected. I am definitely seeing that with the Zoom twelve-step meetings. And when all of this is over, and we can gather once again in a church basement (I never thought I would miss that so much . . . and the bad coffee. I even miss the bad coffee), it will be so weird to shake hands. When we can, I am going to be on the other side now. I will be the one standing at the door outstretching my arm first to everyone who attends, because there will be a lot of people coming out of their dark basements for the first time, and I want them to have the same connection that welcomed me so many years ago. But for now, we will all get through this one virtual handshake at a time.

Natalie Harris currently serves as a councillor for the City of Barrie, Ontario. She is the author of Save-My-Life School: A First Responder's Mental Health Journey *and the mother of two beautiful children, Caroline and Adam. Natalie is proud to be the grandmother to baby Beckham and has three fur babies.*

SOLIDARITY IS NOT CANCELLED

BY HEATHER DOWN WITH DIMITRI NEONAKIS

EARLY FALL WAS YOUNG DIMITRI'S favourite time of year. He loved watching the crop-duster planes swoop and dive low over the olive trees on his home island of Crete. Flying fascinated him.

At the age of nineteen, Dimitri would end up in Nova Scotia, forging a new life, building a family, and sharpening an entrepreneurial spirit. Although still intrigued by aviation, Dimitri developed a fear. His anxiety grew, and he approached his doctor about the issue.

"Doctor, I am not sure what I should do. I have a real fear of flying."

The doctor suggested that to manage his phobia, maybe Dimitri could avoid commercial flights, at least for a little while. But Dimitri was not sure that was the best way to face hardship. He wanted to do something—he *needed* to do something—to tackle his emotions, a trait that would stay with him.

He decided to fight fire with fire. He knew that knowledge was everything, so he signed up for flight lessons. He worked through his training to get his private pilot's license. It was hard, almost impossible at first, but he faced his fear straight on. It was his way to cope, and it did not take long for him to conquer his anxiety.

Then on April 18 and 19, 2020, Nova Scotia faced a tragedy of unimaginable proportion. A deadly killing spree spanning time and distance—homes were burned, victims were murdered. It shook the country to its core. This was a crisis of epic proportion compounded by another crisis—COVID-19. Social distancing changed the face of how people were allowed to grieve and comfort each other.

This broke Dimitri's heart. He wanted desperately to go to Portapique and embrace those people and say, "Hey, what can I do?" But he was unable. Times were different.

So he decided to jump into his airplane, a Cirrus, with his partner, Lara, and go for a flight. It was a spontaneous decision.

Dimitri needed to do this to comfort himself. He needed to once again face his emotions. He wanted to hug the whole community of Portapique from the air and circle them and, in his own mind, say, "I love you. I support you. I am with you. We are in this together. We are going to get through this."

Dimitri radioed the Halifax tower. "This is Charlie Golf Zulu Papa Tango asking clearance for takeoff."

The air traffic controller responded, "Where are you headed?"

"North."

"What is the purpose of your trip?" she inquired.

"Sightseeing," he responded.

The controller cleared him for takeoff.

Dimitri took off. It was one of the most quiet and peaceful flights of his life. Both he and Lara were silent. As he flew over Portapique, the pain was palpable. He could feel the collective grieving, the destruction, and he knew no one would know he was above them on this mission. He did not have smoke trailing behind him, nor had he told anyone of the specific shape of his flight pattern. Yet he felt the sentiment of thousands of people with him in the cockpit, offering condolences and love.

An hour later, Dimitri landed back in Halifax and was instructed to exit the runway and follow a certain taxi path to his parking spot. Before saying goodnight, the air traffic controller said, "That was a beautiful thing you did."

Stunned, he answered, "Yeah? You saw that?"

Of course she did, he thought. With the decreased air traffic due to COVID-19, there was only one controller, and she would have seen him on the radar the whole time he had meticulously flown a heart-shaped path over a province in mourning.

When Dimitri returned home, he realized that someone had posted the flight radar online, and it had gone viral. He returned to a plethora of messages and media requests. He felt conflicted. He was simply a man grieving; he was not seeking attention, especially when so many others were suffering so deeply and facing such devastating loss. He wanted to decline all requests.

The next day he called his daughter in California, who changed his mind. "Dad, right now everything is so negative on the TV and in the news. Your story is a glimmer of hope. People need a story like this right now."

Upon reflection, Dimitri agreed.

For Dimitri personally, this was the most meaningful flight he had ever taken. Although the heart-shaped flight path was flown for Dimitri's benefit, it became something bigger, something more. It was a glimmer of hope in times when everyone and everything seemed hopeless, in a time when people had to grieve alone, in a time when senseless evil ravaged a community, and in a time when a tiny virus attacked the world. When you don't think anybody is noticing, sometimes the smallest gesture can have the biggest impact.

Dimitri Neonakis is an entrepreneur who lives in Dartmouth, Nova Scotia. He is passionate about flying and giving back.

A GARDEN OF HEARTS IS NOT CANCELLED

BY CATHERINE KENWELL

"CONSTRUCTION PAPER," CHECK.

"Scissors." Check.

"Sharpies." Check.

"Bamboo sticks." Check.

Not exactly the type of tools you'd expect to use when combatting COVID-19. But these are the items I assemble on the coffee table while I'm watching the morning news and listening to the latest developments on the coronavirus.

I sip my coffee and get to work. It's been a long time since I cut out hearts, and my scissors follow what I hope is an adequate path to something that resembles heart shaped. I create one, then two, and another two. They're uneven, but they look like hearts.

We're going to be stuck inside for a while, apparently. Today the government has told us to avoid unnecessary travel and to maintain at least two metres between us when we're outside.

So we can walk the dog, but we can't congregate with our extended family. We can say hello to neighbours, but we can't drop in for a visit.

I keep cutting, sipping coffee, listening to the news while I work. I have nineteen hearts.

Now, I employ the black Sharpie.

"You are beautiful!" I write. "Look at you with your COVID hair, you're gorgeous!"

I print what I hope will be inspiration, a little drop of good cheer during this dismal time.

"Hello!"

"Keep healthy!"

"Wash your paws!"

"Give us your most beautiful smile!"

"Do your silly dance!"

"Hop on one foot to the next house!"

And then, my family's favourite, "If we can smell your farts, you're standing too close!"

Carefully, I attach bamboo sticks to each brightly coloured heart. These little crafts, they look like the work of children instead of a fifty-eight-year-old. They're imbalanced, messy, imperfect.

I pull on my boots and open the front door. My arms are filled with nineteen paper hearts on sticks.

One by one, I place them. In the front garden, near the sidewalk, I push the sticks into soft soil. They're placed so that anyone can read them as they walk by. I fail to realize that the last one in the row is the "fart" heart, and most onlookers seem to take a moment longer to read that one. And then laugh. Or maybe they are grimacing at the uncouth comment. Sometimes I can't tell.

What a joy it's been, watching people of all ages enjoying something so simple. Hearing from neighbours we had yet to meet. Saying hello. It's even been laugh-inducing, witnessing little dogs lifting their legs against them.

We're living in extraordinary times, when every day we are unsure about how to live our lives. We're afraid, and depressed, and we have cabin fever. Everything—and every day—seems wrought with new challenges and rules. It's exasperating.

If we hadn't been home isolating, we wouldn't have moved my office to the second floor.

And if we hadn't moved my office, I wouldn't have discovered the stash of neon-coloured construction paper.

And if I hadn't found the paper, none of this would have happened.

Sometimes it's the most unremarkable chain of events that leads to something extraordinary.

And sometimes the extraordinary is not extraordinary at all; maybe it's simple and messy and imperfect. Just like our little garden of hearts.

KINDNESS IS
NOT
CANCELLED

BY HEATHER DOWN WITH MICHELLE HEDGES

MICHELLE IS AN OCCUPATIONAL THERAPIST, an essential worker providing psychotherapy to clients living in a community about a forty-minute commute from her home. She is doing her best to go out for groceries only once a week. One day she decided to take her lunch hour early at 10 a.m. and buy groceries because the lineup outside the grocery store at noon was always ridiculous. In addition, she had some clients booked throughout the actual lunch hour.

The line waiting to enter the store moved quickly, and soon Michelle was inside, doing her shopping. A strange phenomenon had occurred since the pandemic hit. Lately, she found shopping more peaceful. Unlike before, when it felt like a mindless task, racing through her day and quickly grabbing groceries, a certain mindfulness had developed. Everything seemed to slow down, people exhibited more patience, and folks appeared to really notice each other. Even though there was physical distancing, a connection was growing and flourishing.

After she had scanned her groceries at the self-checkout, Michelle realized she had left her bank card at home. Suddenly she was knocked out of her new-found Zen-like shopping experience and back into the default of worrying about things that, when considered with perspective, didn't really matter in the great scheme of things: having only an hour for her lunch, having to race back to work, and not knowing how she would pay for the groceries.

With just a clerk and another customer nearby, Michelle started narrating aloud, trying to figure out her options. "Oh, no. I'm not really sure what to do. I forgot my bank card. I am an essential worker, and I just used my lunch hour to gather groceries that I won't be able to buy."

A woman came over and tapped her card to pay for the eighty dollars' worth of groceries.

Michelle wanted to somehow pay her back. However, the lady refused. She told Michelle to not worry about it.

Michelle didn't know how to respond. She stood there a bit confused. At first, she felt guilty because she considered herself one of the lucky ones to still have a job. Then the guilt melted to feeling silly because she had forgotten her bank card.

The cashier suggested, "Maybe you could pay it forward."

Michelle thanked the kind stranger again before leaving the store, promising the generous lady that she would pass on the gift. She briefly considered waiting for the woman to come out to thank her again and plead for her email address so she could transfer her money. But instead, she allowed the idea of paying it forward to simmer. Even though she may not have needed financial assistance with her groceries, she realized the emotional support from someone who simply had the back of a struggling stranger was a gift she needed to accept.

She went back to work and shared the story with her co-workers, bringing a few of them to tears. Michelle also texted her family, telling them what had transpired. After finishing a therapy session, her phone lit up. Her brother and sister and their families had each donated eighty dollars to their local food banks and her father, a hundred—they were paying it forward on Michelle's behalf.

Michelle's family had been pretty isolated from each other because of the pandemic. This was especially difficult as Michelle's mom had passed away in November, and they all missed her dearly. Her parents had been together for over forty years. Her father's text read: **Boy, Mom and I brought up some great kids. Now stop making me cry. Love, Dad.**

This act of kindness was more than just a connection between two strangers; it also reconnected Michelle to her family, and especially, to her late mom's presence and influence. A gift she cherished.

Michelle wanted to complete the circle. She pondered what she personally could do, and then she realized what that something special would be: she purchased some bracelets for her family members from 4ocean, a charity that helps clean oceans of plastic debris. It was her mother's favourite cause, and it seemed the perfect way to connect her mother into the situation. After all, her mother's positive influence in her children's lives had made them who they are today.

That one small act of kindness had a far-reaching impact—from those receiving food from the food banks to the renewed connection of a family to fond memories of a lost loved one to an ocean that has a little less garbage in it—all because someone made the split decision to lend a hand to someone struggling.

Michelle Hedges works in the field of mental health. She lives in central Ontario and appreciates the power of kindness.

MAKING NEW FRIENDS IS NOT CANCELLED

BY JILL O'CRAVEN

IT'S TWO WEEKS INTO ISOLATION, and I'm running out of food. Not all food, not yet—I still have plenty of chips and cookies and pasta—but the fresh fruit and vegetables are long gone, and the frozen ones are down to their last dregs. I need a grocery run. It's nerve-wracking, leaving the house. It's only the fourth time I've gone outside in two weeks—and two of those were to the compost pile around the side of the house. I have become a recluse, not to mention nocturnal, sleeping all day and hiding in my room all night, emerging only to use the bathroom or find food.

And now, I must find food farther afield.

Planning to go out feels like preparing for battle. I map routes, consider timing, wonder if I should Uber or try to bike. I pack only bags that can be washed, put my towel in the bathroom so I can shower as soon as I return home.

And I text my friend Emily, who just celebrated the five-year anniversary of her heart transplant, who is on immunosuppressants, who is living alone with her cat and her chronic illnesses and has not touched another human being in longer than I can imagine. Going out for groceries. Do you need anything? I can bike them down to you tomorrow.

She asks me for chicken and fresh fruit, and I oblige, glad to be able to provide her with connection and resources in this frenzied time. The chicken has a sign saying ONE PER CUSTOMER, but after a quick chat with a store employee whose brother has diabetes, I add a second package to my cart. The longer Emily's supply can last, the less she has to interact with the outside world, the better.

The next day, I bike down to Emily's apartment. It rained overnight and will rain again in the evening, but for the moment it is beautiful and clear and surprisingly warm for Canada in March.

I pull up in front of the building and see Emily's cat watching me from the window. I wave, smiling, and text Emily: I'm out front.

I'm still waiting when another person approaches the building. She cradles a tiny puppy in one arm and a basket of treats (human treats, not puppy treats) in the other. We smile in greeting, six careful feet apart. I look again to Emily's cat and notice the new person is looking at her, too.

"She's my friend's cat," I say, wondering if the woman thinks I live here or that I wave to strangers' cats all the time (to be fair, I might).

"She's my sister's cat!" the woman says. "Nice to meet you! I'm Rebeccah."

"Oh, wow!" I say. "I'm Jill. I've texted Emily; she's on her way down."

"Perfect," Rebeccah says. "She doesn't know I'm coming—I wanted to surprise her. I was picking up the puppy here in town, and so I decided to drop off a care package and introduce them."

A moment later, Emily opens the door. She spots me and smiles. Then she sees Rebeccah and her jaw drops. And then she sees the puppy, and she melts, sitting down hard on the front step.

"You're here!" she says, stunned. "You're here. What?"

Rebeccah laughs, setting the puppy on the ground between her and Emily. Emily reaches out, making encouraging noises as the puppy takes a few tentative, clumsy steps, and Emily scoops her up.

She buries her face in her fur, hands shaking. "She smells so good," she says. "But you . . . what . . . how . . ."

"She's nine weeks old," Rebeccah says, still laughing. "We're thinking of calling her Gimli."

"We figured out we both knew you when we were admiring your cat," I say, laughing, too. I unshoulder my bag of supplies and lay it a few feet away before moving back out of range. "I brought your groceries."

"And I brought you some treats," Rebeccah says, setting the basket beside it.

"And a puppy!" Emily says.

"And a puppy," Rebeccah agrees.

We stay like that for a few moments, trading stories and questions and adoring looks at Gimli. But none of us can stay long. Emily isn't dressed for the weather, unseasonably warm as it is. Rebeccah has a long drive home. It's getting dark, and I haven't charged my bike light since November.

We trade goodbyes mixed with promises to call soon and to meet up for coffee when this is all over. And then I walk away, from friends and sisters and cats and puppies. But as I bike back to my half-empty house, legs burning from the first exercise I've gotten in weeks, my heart feels full.

Jill Annika O'Craven is a listener, learner, reader, and writer who has never met a written medium she didn't like. She is an editor for Her Campus Western *and has been published in* Iconoclast, Snaps, *and the* Western Gazette. *She also runs the Facebook page Stories Cut Short, which she founded in June 2016.*

SUPERHEROES ARE NOT CANCELLED

By Stephanie Wood with Robbie Griffiths

KEEPING THE ATTENTION OF A one-year-old is a challenge at the best of times. By nature, small children are easily distracted and their focus consistently fleeting, a fact observed by Robbie Griffiths as he stood on a ladder outside a front window, trying to capture the intrigue of a little boy named Logan—the son he couldn't touch.

As a full-time essential worker with Loblaw's during the pandemic, necessary precautions and daily window visits had taken the place of physical contact between Robbie and his pride and joy, and without the ability to lift Logan up into the air or induce a belly laugh by hiding and scaring his mom, the father found himself at the end of one visit in particular at a loss, but with an idea. Back at home, previously worn for select birthday parties and charity events, was a suit, and now felt like just the right time to put it back on. It could take his mind off everything that was going on around him, and perhaps in doing that, he could bring a smile or two to someone else. Maybe even his son would be curious about his alter ego.

"Okay, I'm going to dress up as Spider-Man and go for a walk," he announced through the glass, to the amusement of his son's mother.

"Really?"

"Well, I've got nothing better to do and if anyone sees me, it'll probably give them a laugh!"

An outfit change and a Facebook post announcing his plans later, Robbie set off on his very first patrol, returning full circle to the ladder, the window, and an ebullient Logan, who could not contain his excitement when the masked man revealed himself to be his dad—the mark of a successful day in the life of a superhero.

Also waiting for Robbie at the end of his journey? Two hundred messages from parents in the community, hoping to secure a sighting of Spider-Man for their housebound children.

ACROSS TOWN, ROBBIE WASN'T THE only Paradise, Newfoundland, resident seeking new and interesting ways to positively occupy a mind with a case of cabin fever. As a childminder for an essential worker and a mother of two boys of my own, I hold onto a firm belief that we, as adults, have a responsibility to our children in these uncertain times. The black mark of COVID-19, I decided early on, was not going to mar the childhood landscape of those in my charge. There would be no talk of death or unemployment rates within the earshot of tiny humans. While the six feet of snow in our backyard (a painful reminder of January's infamous "Snowmageddon") made outside play unappealing to us all, we would make our own fun inside. There were science experiments to perform, Easter eggs to colour, and plenty of crafts and baking to partake in, and it was during a browse through Facebook groups for fresh ideas that I happened upon a Paradise Community Group post shared by a friend: a picture of Robbie Griffiths, our apparent friendly neighbourhood Spider-Man, strapped into his car and giving a peace sign.

Friendly neighbourhood Spiderman here, I'm out and about walking some streets in Paradise. If you have kids that would be excited to see Spiderman out walking around their area, let me know the street and I'll make my way to the area. Remember, always six feet apart, be safe, and have fun.

The post had two hundred comments.

"Darren, have you seen this?" I asked my husband, turning my screen toward him. "There's a guy in a Spider-Man costume literally patrolling the streets of Paradise for the kids."

"What a cool idea! You know who would lose his mind over that, right?" he replied with a nod before turning back to the news.

Toby, our four-year-old, lives and breathes for Marvel's resident web-slinger. His walls are adorned with canvas comic book covers, an homage to the hero he hopes to someday become if he continues practising his signature pose, and while it seemed a comment from me on this Facebook post, with a plethora of enthusiastic and hopeful responses from other parents hoping to catch a glimpse of our hero, would get lost in the shuffle, as Toby's mother, I owed it to him to toss our street into the ring.

This is incredible! I've got four kids here in Elizabeth Park that would absolutely lose their melons over a Spidey sighting—hat's off to you, sir!

One week later, on a frigid Sunday afternoon, I would have the privilege of watching Robbie Griffiths in action.

"TOBY, SWEETHEART, HE ONLY STARTED doing his patrol at two o'clock," I explained to the petite boy in a Spider-Man winter coat and hat as I shivered on the front step. We had been in the driveway for over an hour, and even with his mittens on, I was certain he had to be feeling the chill. "He still has a lot of streets to go to before he gets to ours. Why don't we go inside and wait?"

"No, Mommy. I'm actually not even cold!"

The exciting announcement had come that morning: Spider-Man would be heading out to make his rounds. The very last street on his list for the day was ours, a fact that did not deter my son from taking up a position outside long before any chance of seeing his hero was a possibility. In shifts, my husband and I supervised his watch for hours, until finally a slender figure in red appeared on the horizon.

"Toby, look! Look down the road!" my husband alerted him, and Toby sprang into action, abandoning the scooter he had been playing with and scrambling up the snowbank on our front lawn, crouching down atop the icy hill with his arm and hand out-stretched. "Bo, what are you doing?! Can you see him?"

Looking back over his shoulder, Toby exclaimed with delight, "He came to our house! It's Spider-Man!"

Robbie was still quite some distance away, but he'd spotted the little boy perched in a pose he knew all too well, waving and waiting to be noticed. "Hi! I love your hat!" He smiled beneath his mask as he came closer, ducking down and mirroring the stance from the other side of the street. Acknowledged by his idol, Toby giggled and pushed himself clumsily to his feet, bouncing with delight as we looked on in awe.

"Are you having fun playing in the snow?" Robbie called to him, taking steady strides toward him.

"Yeah! Come closer!"

Physical distancing, an integral part of the management of COVID-19, might have prevented Toby from giving him a high-five, but Robbie, we discovered, would still find a way to turn an encounter from six feet away into something special.

"Do you know how to do any dances?" Robbie called, standing tall across the road. "Can you do the floss?"

He began swinging his arms, and from his position on the snowbank, Toby followed suit. "There you go!" Robbie encour-aged as the enchanted little boy did his best to keep up with the movements, hips swaying and arms flailing, passers-by joining us in warm laughter as they stumbled upon the scene, waving as Rob-bie returned to his patrol with a hearty, "Keep safe, guys!"

As I watched him disappear out of sight that day, my son calling after him to come back, I couldn't help but wonder if Robbie Griffiths, a man I had never truly met, had the slightest idea of the profound impact he was making on our community during this difficult time. While walking the streets of our town as a recognizable superhero certainly made people smile, which was the intended outcome, his actions will shape the way the children he's visited remember what will be written about in history books as one of the darkest times of our generation. The daily updates, the quarantine, the anxiety, and the stress facing parents who feared illness and job losses and the future—these are not the things these children will recall in any great detail. When they are grown and their own children ask, "What do you remember about COVID-19?" ours will likely respond, "Well, I remember meeting Spider-Man!"

To the man behind the mask, thank you. You and the light you brought us in darkness are what my family, and so many others you've touched, will remember about COVID-19 in Newfoundland.

Born in Alberta and raised in Newfoundland, Stephanie Wood is a wife, a mother, and a writer. She lives in Paradise and is up to her eyeballs in children and laundry. She awakens daily questioning her life choices, hoping to make it through the third page of the poetry book she started reading in the summer of 2019.

When Robbie Griffiths isn't playing Spider-Man, he is busy being an essential worker and a father to Logan.

Photo credit: Rhonda Fleming

FOND MEMORIES ARE NOT CANCELLED

BY CATHERINE KENWELL

TODAY'S DOG WALK TOOK US up our street and down memory lane. As the dog and I peered into our neighbours' front windows, we witnessed the bright posters and feel-good messages that are meant to keep spirits up and to distract kids from the fear of COVID-19.

Our next-door neighbour, for example, has hoisted a massive white bear into the front window. Its chubby, cheery ursine face is a welcome sight for kids passing by in strollers or riding their shiny spring trikes alongside their parents. This teddy bear initiative is based on a kids' book called *We're Going on a Bear Hunt*. The idea is that kids will hope to spot bears while they're taking a break from being stuck inside their houses.

On the sighting of our third bear, I smiled. Bittersweet. A memory. God, my mom would be the biggest hero right now. She'd be at the front of the line to display her plush bears in the window, no doubt making kids throughout the city thrilled with their augmented bear count.

Oh, my mom had every stuffed bear you could imagine.

Personally, I had given up teddy bears and plush animals when I was about twelve, and I considered her attraction to them infantile. I figured she was likely replaying some unfulfilled childhood need. She was, after all, an in-the-middle child in a family of nine, and it was during the Depression, so perhaps teddy bears were at a premium and she lost out. However, the collection secretly disgusted me. I thought they were a stupid waste of time and money and a forest's worth of dust collectors.

My father would buy my mom anything she wanted, so the bear collection grew to, I'm estimating, forty or so. They lined the back of the chesterfield; they were on their bed and scattered throughout other rooms. They hung on walls and from lamps.

They were even in the bathroom—of course, they matched the princess-perfect retro purple tiles and toilet. Those bears never poop in the woods.

For Valentine's Day, a white plushie would appear, holding a satin heart and a carnation. For Easter, a mauve or pale-yellow bunny plush accompanied her Easter card. When my parents moved from their house to an apartment, I thought for sure some of those bears would be adopted out. But no. Each one resumed its place in the new abode. The small purple bear still hangs in the apartment bath, although my mom's been gone five years and my dad is not a collector.

We used to tease her relentlessly about her bevy of bears. We'd prank her by turning them all on their heads. We'd hide them or put them in compromising positions. We tormented her, and she good-naturedly accepted it. Over time, her bear collection became her silent, stalwart army; the grandchildren were discouraged from playing with them. To us, they were mute troops standing ready to go to war at any moment.

If my mom were here today, she'd be ninety-three; gosh, those bears . . . what memories . . . what fun . . . what love. How I miss her eccentricities. I'm growing more like her, and it's startling how much I'm starting to take on her facial expressions.

I miss my mom.

I wonder what she'd do during this pandemic. My dad says she'd be a nervous wreck. I dare to disagree; I think she'd be setting up her ursine army, trying to give every kid in the world something to smile about. Oh yeah, she'd be the leader of the pack.

And this kid? Her kid? Me? Yep, I'm smiling. With a bittersweet tear in my eye. She's five years gone, and I still want to give her one more hug. Well . . . after this is all over, anyway. Meanwhile, I'm gonna keep looking for bears.

KARMA IS NOT CANCELLED

BY HEATHER DOWN WITH ROBIN STEVENSON

BACK IN 2015, IN VICTORIA, BC, Robin's friend Janet led a group to answer the call to sponsor a Syrian refugee family. Robin, her partner, her parents, and her eleven-year-old son were eager to be a part of this opportunity. Robin's parents, Ilse and Giles, had spent time in Syria and had friends there, which perhaps made them feel all the more connected to the heartbreaking events that were taking place. Robin had been doing some fundraising within the Canadian kid lit community for Doctors Without Borders but wanted to do something more.

The group spent six months fundraising: they needed to raise enough money to support a family of six for their first year in Canada. They also had to find housing and collect furniture, household items, four car seats, toys, strollers, and so on. And they needed to make a plan to prepare for the arrival of the family.

The day finally came when the group would meet their sponsored family at the airport. They were excited to greet the young couple, Marwa and Salem, and their four children. The smallest child was just a few months old and the oldest only six. The travellers had had a very long journey, so they didn't visit for long that day. The group took the refugees to their new home to let them rest. Over the next weeks and months, though, they spent a lot of time together—going to appointments, setting up bank accounts, helping get the kids enrolled in school and the parents in English classes, and, of course, becoming friends in the process.

The family soldiered forward, forging life in their new country, and about a year ago they opened a local store called Damascus Market. They sell a variety of groceries, many organic, including such products as dried beans, coffee, olives, milk, chicken, beef, and fresh fruit and vegetables.

In early March, Robin's family left for Mexico when the only travel advisories were warnings not to travel to China, Italy, and Iran. Robin's son's school had a group going to Japan, but her son, now fifteen years old, decided he'd rather go to Mexico. So off the family went. A few days later, Canadians were advised not to travel, COVID-19 was classified as a pandemic, and then Canadians were advised to return home. Robin's family weren't able to get an earlier flight back, so they kept their scheduled flights. They were very anxious to be back in Canada.

As flights started to get cancelled, worry increased about the possibility of being stuck in another country. The family weren't concerned about having to self-isolate—they just wanted to get home!

When she finally arrived back safely to her house to self-isolate, Robin relaxed. They hadn't expected to be in this position and realized they needed to figure out how to get someone to bring them groceries.

Then the doorbell rang. Robin answered it and was so surprised. She looked down to see bags and bags of groceries at her door. A few metres away, she saw Marwa and her family, safely practising social distancing. Robin was deeply moved by the thoughtfulness and generosity and was grateful for Marwa's help. Robin wanted to give her a hug but instead shouted her thanks from a safe distance away.

Robin couldn't help but reflect on how much refugees contribute to the communities they resettle in. Canada is better because of them—stronger, kinder, more diverse. Resettlement is important for humanitarian reasons—and life-changing or even life-saving for many refugees—but it also benefits Canada tremendously.

Over the past few years, Robin has had the opportunity to participate in four more sponsorships and has become friends with many newcomers—and her life is so much richer because of them. She took a moment to be grateful not only for the groceries that sat before her but also for having such thoughtful, smart, and compassionate people in her life.

Robin Stevenson is an award-winning author of more than twenty-five books for kids and teens. Her writing has been translated into a number of languages, published in more than ten countries, and has won or been nominated for numerous awards. She writes both fiction and non-fiction, for toddlers through teens.

HILARITY IS NOT CANCELLED

BY CHRISTINE NEWMAN

MY STANDARD MORNING ROUTINE IS scanning headlines in the news while waiting for that first cup of coffee from my coffeemaker. A headline on CBC and BBC caught my eye about Canadians being kind during these stressful times.

I started looking for other examples of kindness in the days to come. A friend in uniform sent me a photo that another officer in their division had taken from the car window when stopped to fill out a report: one of those gigantic stuffed teddy bears that you see in midway booths, the kind that takes both people on a date to carry home. This teddy bear was on a balcony, wearing a homemade face mask with a big sign in front that said FREE AIR HUGS. Just the thing to cause a smile.

Or stopping into a local store where I buy my crossword puzzle books and other items. It's near my favourite coffee shop, and I have been shopping there since I moved to the neighbourhood seven years ago. As I was paying for my puzzles, lottery tickets, and cigarettes, the owner slipped a package of five face masks into my bag, and when I looked at him, he said, "So you can stay safe when you have to go out." I was about to step away from the counter when his wife stopped me to put a couple of squirts of hand sanitizer in my hands before I left. "Just to stay safe," she said. That's why I love going to the little mom-and-pop shops.

You quickly get used to the new way of doing things, like grocery shopping every two weeks versus popping out as you need something. To keep physical distancing possible, only a certain number of shoppers are allowed in the store at a time, so folks line up from the entrance, around the parking lot, and sometimes out to the sidewalk, keeping two metres minimum distance. I'm waiting in line, catching up on some emails and text messages on my phone, when I hear from behind me, "Well, holy cow, would you look who decided to show herself in the daylight!" I turn around to find a friend from a local residence for retired artists, and we both have a good laugh. Seeing as we can't do our standard hugs, we both just knew the appropriate greeting, in the style of Robin Williams in *Mork and Mindy*: "nanu nanu" (with the hand gestures, too).

There was grey sky above and not many smiles seen behind all the face masks, so we decided to have a bit of fun while we waited. We bounced a few ideas back and forth and came up with a song for some laughs and some fun while we passed the time. My friend, with a very saucy wink said, "C'mon, kid, let's show this bunch how we have fun," and we started to be two silly, goofy kids in the lineup at the back of the parking lot. It worked—we heard laughter as we got into our routine. Improv and laughter, there's nothing better. I wrote down what I could remember on the back of the cash register tape as I was leaving the store. The lyrics are sung to the tune of "If You're Happy and You Know It."

To be healthy and don't spread it, wash your hands.
To be healthy and don't spread it, wash your hands.
To be healthy and you know it, and you really wanna show it,
To be healthy and don't spread it, wash your hands.
To be healthy and don't blow it, cover a cough. (cough into your sleeve/elbow)
To be healthy and don't blow it, cover a cough.
To be healthy and you know it, and you really wanna show it,
To be healthy and don't blow it, cover a cough.

To be healthy and don't spread it, stay at home.
To be healthy and don't spread it, stay at home.
To be healthy and you know it, and you really wanna show it,
To be healthy and don't spread it, stay at home.

When I'm doing check-ins and peer support with folks on the front lines, my parting piece of advice is always, "Don't forget to find a moment to pause for a laugh today. It's good for you."

And it's truly the Canadian thing to do.

Christine Newman is an author, educator, and speaker. She serves as an LGBTQ2S Peer Support Advisor and Lived Experience Facilitator for the Mood Disorders Society of Canada Peer and Trauma Support Systems team. Known to her loved ones as a certified comical curmudgeon, she loves a good laugh and has missed petting every dog she meets.

DELIVERIES ARE NOT CANCELLED

BY HEATHER DOWN WITH BRIAN GENEAU AND DAVID HALE

MIRAMICHI IS A STUNNING NEW Brunswick city, boasting a picturesque river dividing the two previously named towns of Newcastle and Chatham. The now amalgamated city also boasts two Pizza Delight franchises, which are situated on opposite sides of the Miramichi River.

David Hale owns the franchise on the Newcastle side and Brian Geneau owns the one on the Chatham side. Although they may work on separate banks, these community-minded business owners bridged their thoughts and resources to create a plan to support the staff of the Miramichi Regional Hospital.

The first week that things shut down because of the coronavirus, Brian mentioned to his wife over breakfast, "We've gotta do something."

In these uncertain times, surely the staff at the hospital would be feeling it the most. He phoned the hospital and the receptionist transferred him to the HR department. "Hi. My name is Brian and I'm from the Chatham Pizza Delight," he began. "I'd like to do something. How about we feed your staff?"

Appreciative, the woman on the other end of the line said, "Okay. So which floor?"

Brian responded, "No . . . no, no, no. Everybody from the person pushing the broom, swinging the hammer, changing the sheets. Everyone."

"You do realize that is hundreds and hundreds of people?"

Brian didn't know how many people there were, but it really didn't matter because he just wanted to do something. With almost thirty years in the restaurant business, he knew that food equals joy. He had the food, so why not spread a little joy in hopes of increasing the morale of the hospital staff?

Brian called David, the other Pizza Delight franchise owner in Miramichi. After explaining his idea, Brian asked, "Do you want to do this? Are you in?" Without hesitation he responded, "Yes, whatever we have to do."

Brian figured he would make between fifty and sixty party-sized pizzas, which was a big but manageable task. However, that plan was thwarted by a subsequent call to the hospital.

"Jeez, I don't know how to tell you this, Brian," Charlene, the hospital representative, began. "We have a problem."

"What's the problem?" Brian asked.

"Because of health precautions, we cannot accept party pizzas. I am sorry." Her voice trailed off.

"Well, what's the solution?" Brian continued.

"I don't want to take advantage of your kind offer . . ."

"No. What is it? What is it that you are saying?"

"The only way we could accept the pizzas would be if they were personal-sized."

"We'll do nine-inch individual pizzas then . . . yep, whatever you need."

Each pizza would have to be self-contained to meet the obligatory requirements for the health and safety of the hospital staff.

Another hurdle was the various floors and shifts, night and day. Both pizza-joint owners got to work on a massive three-day process of making and delivering hundreds of individual pizzas. Making sure to provide food to the largest number of shift workers, they delivered them at different times of the day and night. All in all, about 700 pizzas made their way there.

After all, folks here pride themselves on looking after their neighbours. And hospital staff in a small town are basically on every block and every street, making them an integral part of the community, not only by virtue of their profession but also because they are someone's neighbour, someone's friend.

It felt good to help, but the feedback for both Brian and David was overwhelming. A friend of David's, whose wife was a nurse, said, "Hey, listen, what you guys did for the hospital over there . . . you have no idea how much that pumped them up and how it lifted their spirits."

A few days later, a hospital worker popped in to pick up a personal order at the Newcastle store. "Thank you very much for what you did. You went above and beyond," he mentioned.

The emotional responses from grateful hospital workers didn't stop. Statements of gratitude were an everyday occurrence.

But that sense of community extended beyond just feeding the hospital staff. Brian knew he could do more. He called the manager of the local Sobeys. "Hey, are you doing deliveries right now?"

"No, unfortunately we don't have the staff or means at the moment to offer deliveries."

"Well, we have three drivers going here. Just offer it, and we'll pick up and deliver the groceries to your customers for free."

David, who has owned his Pizza Delight for "half a lifetime," doesn't see what this duo did as a grand gesture. Instead, he views it as merely the Canadian way, an attitude of looking out for one another, a sense of community. He feels that what he and Brian did was merely looking out for those people who were looking out for them.

David Hale and Brian Geneau are Pizza Delight franchise owners in Miramichi, New Brunswick.

TRAVELLING ACROSS CANADA IS NOT CANCELLED

BY HEATHER DOWN

I AM THE COLLECTOR OF the worst jokes ever and the curator of the most punishing of puns. I make it my mission to torture anyone who dares to read my Facebook feed by offering a never-ending supply of humour that causes people to groan or to spit out their coffee or to say aloud, "Oh, that was really bad." I look far and wide for this content and pride myself on the outcome and reactions it garners.

I get messages about what I post. Some people have even mentioned they look forward to my strange aggregate of questionable humour. My grown children will occasionally call me when I post something exceptionally bad. "Are you serious?" Charity, my youngest, will say. "Where do you find this stuff, Mom?" It isn't all rotten. My eighty-nine-year-old father will say, "Hey, I like that joke you posted on Facebook." Even my daughter will occasionally share a meme or two from my assemblage of things that make you say, "*Really?!*"

But then a pandemic hit the world. I could no longer self-regulate my emotions, and I see-sawed from optimism to despair. I worried; I didn't worry. I laughed one minute, wept the next. Everything was confusing. A cousin passed away from cancer. No funeral. My aunt in a long-term care facility tested positive for COVID-19. My elderly parents couldn't be visited and lived in relative isolation. I don't know the exact moment it happened, but I stopped posting.

I poured myself into this project, the book you are currently reading. It seemed like the right thing to do. I would interview someone one day and write a narrative about them the next, evenly paced and steady. I filled my days with chatting and writing, possibly changing out of my pyjamas but not likely, repeat.

One Friday, I unintentionally ended up with four interviews scheduled one after the other. It started with Heather Mesher-Brown in Happy Valley-Goose Bay, and then I called the Yukon for the first time in my life and chatted with the most congenial Gurdeep Pandher (who led me to my second ever call to the Yukon to chat with Jordan Lincez). Jordan and I actually had a lot in common—I am a former educator, and he is currently a teacher. We spoke about places we had both frequented in Ottawa and about his time at Base Borden, which is only a few kilometres from where I live. Then I spoke with Indigenous author David A. Robertson. We found out he had done a book reading at Sioux Lookout, the small northern Ontario town where my son-in-law is from. And Mary Janet from Cape Breton—*Mary Janet*—I just love her. From breakfast to supper, I felt like I had been across this country, and I had made a whole bunch of new friends. It was like a therapeutic dose of positivity.

At the end of the day, my friend Matt Heneghan checked in on me via Messenger. The three previous days had been pretty rough, and he was aware I was struggling. In fact, two days earlier, I couldn't force myself out of bed.

Buddy check. How are you doing?

How am I doing? Taking personal inventory, I realized that I felt pretty good.

Actually, I feel energized! I phoned the Yukon for the first . . . and second time ever. I want to go there one day. Oh, and I talked to this guy in Manitoba, and . . .

I proceeded to give him the rundown of my entire day of interviews.

Sounds like travelling across Canada isn't cancelled. You went to all those places while sitting in your home office.

Wow! He was right. I connected with the entire country, east to west, and places in between, making new friends, all while remaining in lockdown. Even isolation couldn't stop me from reaching out and experiencing the different regions this great land has to offer.

Yeah. I never thought of it like that. But you are right!

The next day I got up, fired up the computer, and checked Facebook, sharing a meme that caught my eye:

Most puns make me feel numb
But math puns make me feel number

#IAmBack

Heather Down is a frequent contributor to the online platform Vocal Media. Besides owning Wintertickle Press, she hosts the podcast After the Book Ends, *a show where she chats with Canadian non-fiction authors about their lives after their books are published. You can follow her @winterticklepress and @afterthebookends.*

Photo credit: Jan Frew

FIRST DANCE IS NOT CANCELLED

BY HEATHER DOWN WITH JOSH AND ANASTASIJA DAVIS

ALTHOUGH THEIR RELATIONSHIP IS NOTHING to sneeze at, it began with precisely that—a sneeze.

Achoo!

"Bless you," Josh said as he turned around in his seat to face the culprit sneezer. He was at a youth workers conference in Abbotsford, BC. His gaze lingered slightly longer than it should have, landing somewhere in between noticeable and socially acceptable. He was smitten.

After the session was finished, Anastasija, a.k.a. the phantom sneezer, found Josh in the crowd. "Thank you so much for saying 'bless you,'" she acknowledged. "That was kind of you."

Josh thought, *It was nothing. I am just a good Canadian kid, manners and all.* His brain continued to turn over. *Keep talking to her, Josh. Keep talking to her.*

And talk they did, exchanging numbers and realizing they worked a mere block apart. In a matter of weeks, they were dating.

It didn't take Josh long to realize Anastasija was the one he wanted to spend the rest of his life with. He planned an outdoor proposal on September 21, 2019. The forecast didn't seem to be on board with the idea, however: rain. He meticulously arranged the location and the secret photographer and whispered a little prayer: "Please let the rain break for just a half hour."

While they were sitting in a coffee shop, miraculously, not only did the rain subside but the sun came out too, long enough for Josh to ask Anastasija to step outside for his flawless proposal.

The excited couple started to plan for an April 3, 2020, wedding at a Langley golf course. After making their initial guest list, they tallied 150 guests. After some careful thought, they realized some of those guests would not be able to attend because they lived outside Canada, so they whittled the roster down to 135.

Venue secured, invoice in hand, they had everything planned A to Z. About a month before the wedding, it was apparent that COVID-19 was starting to spread in the world well beyond the borders of China. However, Josh and Anastasija felt their wedding was not in jeopardy.

But doubt started to wiggle its way in when their honeymoon was cancelled. "It's okay," Anastasija said. "We can always reschedule and go on a honeymoon later. There is always Plan B."

Three weeks before the wedding, Anastasija's brother was stranded in Europe. Her sister-in-law, who was going to do most of the decorations, was also stuck. One thing after another kept hitting their wedding plans. "There is always Plan B," Anastasija kept repeating. After all, they could always find someone else to do the decorating, right?

Two weeks before the wedding, the coronavirus and their wedding plans collided, crashing the most organized blueprint into shards. While watching the news, they listened to the proclamation: "Those in British Columbia are not allowed to have gatherings of over fifty people."

Anastasija looked at Josh. "What are we going to do?"

"We will just have to reduce the number of guests to fifty," Josh replied.

They called the venue to see if they could shave their numbers to fifty, only to find out that the golf course could no longer host the wedding.

"Is this Plan C or D?" Anastasija joked as they looked at having a backyard wedding at Josh's parents' house. They could invite about thirty-five family members and close friends and the wedding party and still remain under the fifty-people limit.

Emails went out to family and friends to uninvite them to the wedding. It was a tough thing to do, but Josh and Anastasija knew it was the right thing to do in the face of a pandemic.

A couple of still-invited family members contacted them, some with new babies, others worried that someone they knew was exhibiting symptoms of the dreaded virus. They did not want to potentially risk the safety of themselves or others.

"What is the smartest plan for us?" Josh asked.

They decided on a tiny living room service with a skeletal group of family and friends to witness their nuptials. Another mass email was sent out, including heartbreaking messages to the bridesmaids and groomsmen, telling them they could not attend.

"I feel sorry for our guests," Anastasija mentioned. "At least we know ahead of time what is going to happen when we make a decision. They have been so great to just roll with all the last-minute changes."

The couple moved up their wedding to March 22 because they realized that without a get-together or venue, April 3 was just a date on the calendar. They had each other, they had their parents' blessings, and they had their family. What else was necessary? This was about a marriage, not a wedding. They could have a celebration at a future date.

After the service, with just four people in the limo, the couple travelled to Osprey Village for a few quiet photos of their day.

"I am really thankful for our friends," Josh mentioned as they neared the location to take pictures.

"I know. They have been so understanding. They haven't been judgmental. We are really blessed to have such amazing people in our lives," Anastasija added.

"Roll down your windows," the best man suggested.

They rolled down their windows. Josh noticed that the street was lined with cars.

Darn, he thought. *Another wedding party got here first for pictures. We might have to wait a while.*

But then he recognized someone, and someone else . . .

Completely astounded, the couple looked up and down the lined street filled with balloons, signs, bright colours, and sparklers. They saw those they invited—and even some they hadn't—cheering and clapping, cars honking in support.

Completely overwhelmed, Josh and Anastasija cried. As the limo parked, the couple walked up and down the street, receiving congratulations within a very safe distance from those who loved them. Somehow, someone (no one claimed responsibility) managed to organize a group chat and spontaneously and quickly planned this act of solidarity and support. Even nearby neighbours on the street came out on their balconies to witness this incredible sight.

Out of the crowd a voice bellowed, "Why don't you guys have your first dance?"

They had not planned on having their first dance, especially after having their wedding cancelled—twice!

But coordinated, and as if on cue, everyone turned their radio dial to the same station and cranked up the volume, flooding the air with music. Josh and Anastasija had no choice. They began their first totally unplanned but completely perfect first dance.

It was magical and special, something out of a movie. It was a bride and a groom, a wedding dress and a suit in small-town British Columbia, and it was . . . unforgettable.

Although Josh and Anastasija may have been temporarily disappointed that only a handful of people could witness their vows, little did the pair know that their love was destined to be viewed by more than just 150 guests. With over 40,000 shares on social media (when this was written), their guest list was ultimately much bigger than they could ever have imagined!

Joshua and Anastasija Davis are grateful for whom they believe to be the planner of not only their wedding but also their lives, God. They live in BC and are grateful for their friends, their loving parents, their bridal party of Gregg Mair and Talayna Davis, their church friends who made their day extra special, and those who have been praying for them.

BUILDING A HOME IS NOT CANCELLED

BY JJ DETTMAN

AS THE QUARANTINE STRETCHES ON, this house that I share with my roommates has begun to feel like a home and less like a house I just happen to live in. We are all graduate students. In four years, other people will be living here, and we'll have scattered to the winds, across the continent—or oceans, even. Our friendships will have to take a new form if they are to survive and adapt to the great distances we will find between us. I've witnessed such events before, after undergrad. Some of those friendships remain in a limited capacity, such as a monthly phone call or night out, but most don't. Such is life.

With this foresight, it's hard to shake the quiet yet ever present thought that the current conditions of my life are temporary. My work toward my degree will end soon; so, too, will my tenure in this house, and my social life as I know it will follow. Today's friendships are unlikely to last beyond graduation and certainly not with their current strength. I will no longer share a wall or a kitchen, or even live within twenty minutes of my current friends. A sad realization. I like my friends. Through the right lens, I can rework this premonition toward motivating myself to enjoy the time I do have with them if this time is certain to disappear. Even so, the temporary reality of life in this house leaves me with a cold, emotionally distant frame of mind. A house that I plan to leave soon and view as little more than a roof and a bed cannot be a home.

Before the pandemic swept through the world and the curtains of social distancing segmented our community, my roommates and I would see each other semi-regularly. (Except for the guy I share an office with. I see him all the time.) The four of us study in the same department and have offices in the same building, but during the week I would interact with two of my roommates only intermittently. There's a freedom of schedule afforded to graduate students—a major perk of the research profession—and normally I am desynchronized with that half of the house. During the week I might not see them at all. If we did, it would be light exchanges about daily events, or we'd pick up a longer conversation from a couple nights before and shift it forward thirty minutes. On the weekends, we would go out, and sometimes these plans would involve each other but many times not. Each of us maintains our own individual friend groups. The rarest occasion was for all four of us to stay in and spend Friday or Saturday evenings together. Now, of course, this is the only option for real-life socializing we have.

The first week we abandoned our offices was the most disorienting. Thankfully, we can all do our work remotely so that our thesis projects are uninterrupted, but this says nothing about the rest of our lives. Campus—and the outdoors, at large—is closed, so we cannot take walks across the fields or through the halls for brain breaks and coffee. (No more espresso, either.) At home, if I feel the urge to break from work and walk around, to leave my computer desk, which sits not six feet from my bed, the farthest I can go and remain inside is the kitchen. We have no extra livable space in our house. Such is the reality of being a student in urban southern Ontario. There are four bedrooms, a kitchen, a bathroom, and a squished living room. The whole thing sits on a dark, dank unfinished basement, where all four walls and the floor are made of concrete. (A great spot for a quarantine-proof home gym, as well as a quiet space to write, though.) That first week required us to come to terms with the short leash our moral duty to community safety had placed around our necks. In between sporadic bursts of productivity, we wandered out into the common space—as we would do many times at work—expecting to see our building, or people from our larger group of colleagues and friends. We were stunned, dazed, at the realization that we weren't on campus and couldn't go there or see our friends, because that would put lives at risk. Every relationship beyond the house was now relegated to the digital world—a place full of incredibly powerful tools capable of providing meaningful doses of social engagement with our distant friends and family, no doubt. But digital conversations are weak replacements for the real thing. I knew maintaining my sanity through this quarantine would require socialization in a shared, physical space. I think my roommates and most people would agree.

We each had opportunities to return home to family in the area. By the end of week one, no one had left. No one was making plans to leave. Seems the four of us had come to a tacit agreement. To leave now would be abandonment. The house at anything less than full strength is dysfunctional. Without openly acknowledging it, we decided to face this crisis together and make a home out of this house—or go crazy trying.

Our first and most successful creation has been dinner. To celebrate the passing of the first week, our most culinarily inclined roommate proposed we make pizza from scratch. Knead our own dough. I am adventurous in the kitchen, but only to a certain point—a point that falls well short of making dough or noodles or any of those substrates from scratch. The deterrent is the sheer amount of time required for such cooking. I am only one man, and under normal circumstances, I cook only for myself. There are limited hours within the evening, and I would rather spend them playing games or reading than cooking. But this is a quarantine. No better occasion to roll up my sleeves and try something new.

The result was an overwhelming success. The pizza and the wine tasted great, but that was a small point beside the bigger lesson. Arduous recipes are made trivial with a team effort. Splitting the menial tasks of vegetable and pepperoni chopping, dish cleaning, and wine pouring among the less kitchen-savvy of our group allowed the chef to focus on the creative aspect of the task, which is the real source of joy for him. We all win in this scenario. There was delicious, home-cooked food for all. (The taste of fresh dough, my God.) Throughout the cooking and the eating, there was wine, jokes, laughs a plenty. Once it was all ready, we tuned into the TV to continue through the first season of *The Twilight Zone*—an endeavour we'd started before the quarantine.

We have never in three-plus years cooked dinner together, just the four of us. Our mismatch of schedules did much to prevent that. There's less of an excuse on weekends, I suppose, but still it never transpired. We stuck to an impractical procedure of drafting four individual meals in our kitchen at different times of the night. Personally, I would order takeout just as often as I ate in, and rarely did I actually cook—opting for the effortless frozen pizza instead. By pushing us away from our favourite local burritorie and squishing our schedules together, the quarantine has made group dinners a part of our daily rhythm. Returning to the every-man-for-himself lifestyle now would be a terrible regression.

We followed up the great success of pizza night with performances that included chana masala, chili, stir-fry, fresh butternut squash soup and tuna sandwiches, pasta with a red sauce from scratch, nachos with the works, beef and lentil tacos with pan-baked soft-shell corn tortillas, and homemade burgers grilled on the barbeque in the early spring sun. Contributing proportionate pieces to complex, hearty dishes that taste wonderful is much more rewarding than crafting smaller-sized mediocre dishes by yourself. Dinner is no longer a chore. It's my favourite part of the day.

During all other hours—save for fifteen-minute trips to the grocer—there are four people in the house. It reminds me of when I'd come home from school. After dinner, my roommates and I will improvise a plan for the evening just like when I was a kid, watching hockey with my dad, or movies with my mum, or playing games with my brother. At some point, we'll go off on our own—there is just enough space in our house for privacy—but there is at least an hour in every night that I can count on for some real human contact with my roommates. Sounds like a small thing, but this guarantee grounds me. Before, I might come home and not see my roommates at all for the whole night because they would be working late or out at their own extracurriculars. Put too many of those nights in a row and I start to slide and lose grip on reality.

Sometimes the four of us will play video games in the living room or watch TV and movies, of course. The anarchist, who is the most politically charged and knowledgeable among us, is good for a few rounds of political discourse. Trudeau's daily address will come up if he said anything new or interesting. A personal favourite is a new activity, born during the quarantine. Sometimes, to end the night, we will run Wagner through the surround-sound speakers in our living room, and the knitter will unravel his ball of yarn and add an inch to the end of a rainbow scarf while I scribble thoughts from the last few days into a notebook. (Who am I? The writer, they said.)

The presence of constant company is a comfort I've not enjoyed since I moved away from my parents. While Home is still far away, with my mom, my dad, and my brother, the environment my roommates and I have built here, together, emulates some of the best qualities of family life, in their healthiest form. Times like this reveal to me how fortunate I am to be close with my family, and my roommates, too. Neither are givens.

This isn't to say we've created a utopia. I fought with my parents sometimes. There are stresses my roommates and I would rather keep private than share. We lead our own lives. It's the day-to-day survival and the sanity-maintaining aspects of existence that we fight for together. It's a fight we must prepare for daily and that will consume most of our day, and I know I am better equipped in this home than I would be on my own. That's what's so comforting.

Even though many of my current living conditions are temporary—my studies, my time in this house, the quarantine, even—there are lessons here for a lifetime. When the smoke clears and normalcy returns—whenever that may be—I would do well to remember what my roommates and I had in this quarantine, what it means to build a home.

JJ Dettman is a PhD student in science from Ontario. One of his favourite ways to take a break from science and unwind is with literature. Reading and writing stories is a cherished pastime of his.

Photo credit: Tom Howitt

ACKNOWLEDGMENTS

The creation of this book was both fast and furious. Conception to completion took approximately seven weeks, which for a book is akin to lightning. This project would not have been possible without a wide array of contributions from many gracious people who either wrote narratives or reflections, gave of their time to be interviewed, contributed photos, or sent in emails. The kindness of people astounded us in this process.

This is in no way an exhaustive list, but these are the folks who directly contributed to the content in this book. We cannot begin to let you know how much your involvement meant to us:

Arlene Anderson
Jamie Anderson
Sonya Anderson
Charlie Angus
Andrea Aragon
Donna Baldeo
Jennifer Bardeggia
V Bernard
Mav Blundon
Maria Breen
Elizabeth Corkery
Susan Cruickshank
Anastasija Davis
Josh Davis
Davilee Deal
Rob Dekker
JJ Dettman
Heather Down
James Fisher

Rhonda Fleming
Jan Frew
Susan Gaudet
Brian Geneau
Nikki Glahn
Laurie Gordon
Robbie Griffiths
David A. Hale
Natalie Harris
Michelle Hedges
Teresa Hedley
Matthew Heneghan
Patti Hilton
Shelley Hofer
Betty Hoseman
Tom Howitt
Patrick Hunter
Mandy Johnson
Miriam Kemppainen

Catherine Kenwell
Cheyanna Kidd
Jennifer Lagacy-Shaw
Michael Lasitz
Rob Leathen
Jordan Lincez
Andrea Logan
Janet MacDonald Alexander
Mary Janet MacDonald
Patricia MacDonald
Carter Mann
Tania Marsh
Séan McCann
Jason McCoy
Heather Mesher-Brown
Dimitri Neonakis
Christine Newman
Jill O'Craven
Carina O'Neill
Easton O'Neill
Scarlett O'Neill
Gurdeep Pandher
Father Rico Passero
Erin Paterson

Jim Payetta
Jacqueline Pennington
Jason Price
Maud Revel
Barb Roberts
David A. Robertson
Rene Segura
Tracy Segura
Sri Selvarasa
Mabel Senchuk
Michelle Sertage
Tara Shannon
Suresh Singaratnam
Michele Sparling
Suzi Spelic
Christie Stetson
Robin Stevenson
Courtney Taylor
Dave Thomas
Dr. Sarah Waterston
Jean White
Nancie Wight
Stephanie Wood
Jenni Wuttunee

Photo credit: Heather Down

Photo credit: Patricia MacDonald

CONNECT

Facebook: @WintercticklePress

Instagram: @WintercticklePress

Twitter: @Wintertickle

If you enjoyed this book, you will probably enjoy other titles by Wintertickle Press including:

A Medic's Mind by Matthew Heneghan

Brainstorm Revolution: True Mental Health Stories of Love, Personal Evolution, and Cultural Revolution by Heather Down, Natalie Harris, and Courtney Taylor

Enter Laughing: The Early Years by Neil Crone

Save-My-Life School: A First Responder's Mental Health Journey by Natalie Harris

Stories: Finding Your Wings by Heidi Allen

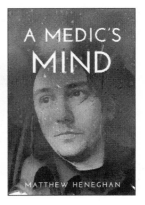